A Climate For Appeasement

Studies in History and Culture

Norman F. Cantor, Editor

Vol. 3

PETER LANG
New York • Bern • Frankfurt am Main • Paris

Terrance L. Lewis

A Climate For Appeasement

PETER LANG
New York • Bern • Frankfurt am Main • Paris

Library of Congress Cataloging-in-Publication Data

Lewis, Terrance L.
   A climate for appeasement / Terrance L. Lewis.
     p. cm. − (Studies in history and culture ; vol. 3)
   Includes bibliographical references.
     1. Great Britain−Politics and government−1936-1945.
2. Great Britain−Foreign relations−1936-1945.   3. Great
Britain−Foreign relations−Germany. 4. Peace movements
−Great Britain−History−20th century. 5. Public
opinion−Great Britain−History−20th century.
6. World, War, 1914-1918−Literature and the war. I. Title.
II. Series.
DA578.L45   1991   941.083−dc20   90-6166
ISBN 0-8204-1314-3   CIP
ISSN 0743-2879

© Peter Lang Publishing, Inc., New York 1991

Printed in the United States of America.

TABLE OF CONTENTS

INTRODUCTION

One of the most written about areas of modern European history is the set of British foreign policies usually known as appeasement. The actions of Stanley Baldwin, Neville Chamberlain, and those who served under them and assisted them in pursuing those policies have been well documented, and perhaps even over-analyzed. Many different theories about the causes and effects of appeasement have been suggested, most going against at least some of the others.

The idea behind this book is the sorting through of this historiographical material by looking at one of the causes suggested by the appeasers themselves in their memoirs: that they had to appease Germany because the British public was not ready to stand up to Germany. Therefore, a look at the climate of British public opinion, as well as the reasons for this set of opinions being held is necessary.

This shall be accomplished by considering some of the strains of British popular culture, as illustrated by what might be called middle-brow literature. In fact, the original stimulus to this work was a passage in Charles Loch Mowat's classic history of interwar Britain, Britain Between the Wars 1918-1940, where he says [on page 537]:

> In 1935...the two dilemmas, peace or war, appeasement or war, had not been reached...reinforcing the policies of evasion was the pacifist movement.... It had many sources. The postwar

> mood of disillusionment had been revived...[in]
> the war novels, plays and autobiographies
> published in the late twenties....

Is there really such a clear connection? It has often been assumed, but has usually just been stated to exist in an offhand manner. It is up to the reader to judge if this study makes the connections clearer–or proves that such general statements mislead the historian from the true causes of appeasement.

There are many people to thank when a project like this one is finished, and I shall not waste the reader's time by thanking them all in print. The few I should like to point out are Dr. W. Warren Wagar of the SUNY University Center at Binghamton, as well as the other professors and friends who encouraged me while I was there, and my other friends, who also encouraged my work, at the SUNY College at Cortland and the College of Charleston, especially Dr. Stuart Knee and Dr. E. Lee Drago. My special thanks to Ms. Pat Johnson, who helped me get all this material from a large pile of typed pages and margin notes onto disks, for easier editing, to Shirley Wajda, ABD at Penn, in that editing, and Linda Radaker, Mike Phillips, and the other people at the Clarion University Computer Center. My final thanks go to my parents and my sister for their support during my entire education and after.

JINGOISM, PROPAGANDA, AND BRITISH MENTALITÉ

The idea that warfare involves the entire nation, including the mobilization of civilians and the domestic economy, is, of course, a commonplace. It must be remembered, however, that this was not the case before 1914. The United Kingdom entered the "Great War" in 1914 with a great deal of patriotic zeal, which can be contrasted with the grim determination of 1939. Such zeal could only have been maintained under the assumptions of 1914, chief of which was the firm belief held by soldiers and civilians alike: the War might be over by Christmas, and could not last much longer than that.

Examples of the patriotism with which the British entered the War are easy to find, and often show the feelings of the crowd as well as those of the young men who rushed off to volunteer.

> ...the London crowds whooped for joy, soldiers commandeered horses from the shafts of carriages.... [1]

> It was 11 o'clock—12 by German time—when the ultimatum expired. The windows of the Admiralty were thrown open in the warm night air. Under the roof from which Nelson had received his orders were gathered a small group of Admirals and Captains and a cluster of clerks, pencil in hand, waiting. Along the Mall from the direction of the

Palace the sound of an immense concourse
singing 'God Save the King' floated in. On this
deep wave there broke the chimes of Big Ben;... [2]

The only privilege I [Harold Macmillan], and many
others like me, sought was...getting ourselves
killed or wounded as soon as possible. [3]

Macmillan and thousands of other young men were quickly granted
the "privilege" they sought. The 100,000 volunteers called for in early
August, 1914, were easily found. In all, nearly 500,000 men enlisted by
mid-September, 1914, and 2,000,000 had volunteered by the time
conscription was finally introduced in 1916.[4]

Why did all these men rush to enlist? Why did they continue to join
up when the War went past the first few weeks and settled into the
stalemate of the trenches? What of the rest of Britain [population 40.8
million in 1911[5]]? Once a person enlisted, he came under military law,
and could be dealt with by tried methods if his enthusiasm for the War
flagged. The question of how to keep up the morale of the general
population was a different matter, as was, until conscription was started
in 1916, the problem of maintaining enlistment rates after the first wave
of patriotism had waned and the War went past that first Christmas. A
related problem was that of convincing neutral countries [especially Italy
and the United States] that the Allied cause was just, and that those
neutral nations should at least aid the Allied Powers [by extending war
credit and selling them war material] while giving the Central Powers as
hard a time as possible. To solve these problems the establishment in

Britain, as well as the other belligerent nations, turned to propaganda. This chapter will consider the propaganda released for British home front consumption during World War I, ending with speculation on the possible connections between official and unofficial propaganda, the reaction to this propaganda, and later attitudes towards war.

From the early days of August 1914, the British people, like the populations of the other warring nations, were encouraged to believe that their nation's cause was not just necessary in terms of policy, but totally just under moral and international law. As in other nations, Britain's academic and spiritual leaders flocked enthusiastically to the support of their nation's cause.[6] A fine example of a scholar giving early support to the War in an "academic" fashion was the well-known Tudor historian A. F. Pollard [Fellow of All Souls' College, Oxford, and Professor of English history at the University of London], who gave a lecture on the causes of the War at University College on October 5, 1914. The lecture was repeated throughout the next few weeks,[7] and was finally printed as a pamphlet entitled The War: its history and its morals in early 1915.[8]

Pollard came out early in the lecture [the first two paragraphs] to fix the blame for the War clearly on Germany.

> We are not at war because an archduke was murdered, but because that occasion for war burst upon one or two powers not disinclined to break the peace....for, if it is true that it takes two to make a quarrel, it is truer that it takes two to keep the peace....
> [I]t is clear...that Austria...would have found a means of escape from the dilemma.... The ulti-

mate cause of the war must be sought in Germany's frame of mind.... [9]

There is no mention by Pollard of the Austrian ultimatum to Serbia; Russian mobilization along the German and Austrian borders before declaring war; the need of both Austria and Russia to avoid further diplomatic humiliations in the Balkans; the alliance systems of Europe or the entente cordiale which morally committed Britain to support France; or any of the other causes which led up to World War I.[10] The causes of the War which Pollard presented throughout his lecture were the German desire for war in general and the political immaturity of the German populace.

Although Pollard attempted to draw some distinction between "German" and "Prussian,"[11] the lecture made sweeping generalizations about German national characteristics and culture. In short, the German people are shown to have wanted war, and perhaps to have needed war as well.

> Peace [to Germans] is war underhand, with its armies of spies...veiled only until der Tag shall come.... "You will always be fools, "wrote a candid German officer to an English friend, "and we shall never be gentlemen." It is more significant that the German would rather be no gentleman than a fool, while the Englishman would rather be a fool than not a gentleman. The one would rather break the rules than lose the game; the other would rather lose the game than break the rules. [12]

While the German government made war on all of Europe because of the Weltanschauung and <u>Kultur</u> of both its leaders and general population, Britain's involvement, according to Pollard, came out of the highest motives.

> ....intervention [Pollard's term for Britain's declaring war on Germany] was a moral and not a legal obligation. It was, therefore, a debt of honour.... We should have suffered ignominy, even if Russia and France had succeeded without our assistance. If they had failed, we should have lost our honour without the miserable compensation of ignoble security. [13]

Even though British fears of Germany are mentioned by Pollard in a general way, the main thrust of the work [and of the genre] is the redemption of British honor by fighting for Belgium and against the morally immature, if not corrupt and certainly ungentlemanly German state. While British defense needs are mentioned, they are given comparatively little play.[14]

The justness of the British cause and the "playing fields of Eton" were not the only sentiments played on during the early months of the war. For some members of the intelligentsia, the appeal could come through some of the new artistic trends. Although Expressionism and Futurism were under-represented in Britain as compared to the Continent,[15] those few who subscribed to these movements had joined in with their comrades across the Channel to support the 1909 Futurist Manifesto, which declared war to be "the only hygiene of the world."[16]

On the more popular side, however, indignation and patriotism took the place of theory.

> [Protest] was...all directed against the insufferable pretensions of the German Empire and the brutal behavior of its marching armies. Indignation was fierce and popular, and everyone was delighted when [Rupert] Brooke, raising it to a higher plane, identified it with patriotism, and simultaneously made patriotism righteous. [17]

> There has been no time like it in Britain's history. Bands pounding down the streets, patriotic songs endlessly sung in music halls, a stream of often brilliantly conceived posters, the poetry of poets like Rupert Brooke, the speeches of politicians and other self-appointed tribunes of the people, not to mention women with white feathers lurking on street corners—all those and more produced a heady atmosphere.... [18]

Contributing to the "atmosphere," it will be noted, were the poems of Rupert Brooke. Brooke was a young [b. 1887] soldier who died on his way to his first battle on April 23, 1915.[19] His early death meant that his "war poems" did not reflect the disillusionment which the poems of the soldiers who fought in the trenches often show [see Chapter II], and his death in the Greek islands, combined with his good looks and poetry, quickly turned him into a Byronic legend.[20] Brooke's most famous poem, "The Soldier," could serve both as his epitaph and as his main claim on the British mind. Its first few lines are perhaps some of the most famous to emerge from the Great War:

If I should die, think only this of me:
That there's some corner of a foreign field
That is forever England. [21]

Not mentioned by most contemporary observers, however, is a third type of early propaganda [the first two being appeals to reason and patriotism]: atrocity literature. The early atrocity literature was mostly concerned with the German invasion of Belgium. The amount of this literature is staggering. Some were openly propagandistic, one of the best examples being a poem in a 1916 collection by "X" called "To the Kaiser."[22] Others tried to be a more official source of information, such as The Barbarians in Belgium, which appeared in early 1915, and was given some legitimacy by a foreword by Carlton de Wiart, the Belgian Minister of Justice. The selections chosen are from the chapter entitled "Old Men and Little Children," and compare well with the more openly propagandistic works.

"Which is the way to Ghent?" the officer in command of a patrol asked a little boy from Tenrath. The poor little creature did not know German, and replied: "I do not understand." To punish him, they cut off his hands which bleed so severely he dies.

[T]wo...boys were watching the Uhlans passing; they were seized and made to run with their arms bound between galloping horses. Their...bodies were found an hour later in a ditch with their knees "literally worn away,"...one had his...chest split open, and both were shot in the head. [23]

Of course the type of treatment the Germans were supposed to have inflicted on nearly every woman they came across figures prominently throughout the work.[24] [For a less lurid account, see the two volume <u>Reports on the Violation of the Rights of Nations and of the Laws of Customs of War in Belgium</u>, which Nothomb claims <u>Barbarians</u> "complements."][25]

The cumulative effect of all this early propaganda was basically threefold: it encouraged men like Brooke and Macmillan to volunteer for a glorious crusade; it gave a sense of pride and righteousness to the volunteer's family; and it often whipped up violent sentiments amongst the general British population.[26] Shops with foreign names were often attacked, especially after newspaper campaigns about the latest German "atrocity."[27] Throughout the War, militant young women did their part by accosting young men in mufti and trying to verbally shame them into joining the armed forces, often handing them white feathers to make the point.[28]

It was, of course, impossible to maintain the feelings of most people at a fever pitch for very long, let alone for over fifty months. During 1915, recruitment dropped off, and although there were still riots by anti-German mobs, such events were in response to events such as the sinking of the <u>Lusitania</u> [and the subsequent press campaigns]. New propaganda devices had to be developed to keep up home front morale in the face of the stalemate and large number of casualties on the Western Front and at the Dardanelles, keep up the large number of volunteers, and prepare the home front for possible hard times if the German submarine threat proved unstoppable.

Anti-German propaganda was kept up throughout the War, much of it along the same lines as the propaganda of 1914-1915,[29] some of it reaching the level of the story of infamous "corpse factory." Accounts of the early stages of the War also came into fashion, the intent being to stimulate the military ardor of the nation by showing the "Great War" as being more heroic than the casualty lists.[30]

The year 1915 had little good news for the British people, and that little had only small long-term effect. For instance, much was made out of Italy's entrance into the War on May 23, 1915, on the side of the Allies, yet its entry may have caused as many problems, both during the War and after, as it solved.[31] Conversely, there was a great deal of bad news. The true start of the war of attrition started on the Western Front, which was inevitable once the trench system was completed in late 1914 [a state of affairs which would last until March, 1918]. The Germans started using poison gas in April, making the conditions at the Western Front even worse than they had been before. On top of it all, the German submarine threat was starting to come into play and the fiasco at the Dardanelles had begun.

Politically in Britain, the Liberal civilians had taken much of the blame for the military and supply mistakes of the previous year. Churchill, who was most involved [and who had more combat experience than most of the senior officers or Conservative members of Parliament], was sacrificed along with some colleagues, and Conservatives and members of the military were brought into the Government on May 26.

The introduction of Conservatives and the military in the Government led to an issue being brought out which was at least as controversial on the home front as the stalemate on the Western Front, the supposed shortage of shells [an issue much like the later "missile gap" of 1960 or the "window of vulnerability" of 1980], or the Dardanelles campaign: conscription. According to A. J. P. Taylor, the whole idea of conscription in 1915 was an error:

> The most startling political development of the year [1915] was the move towards compulsory military service in Great Britain. This was not due to any shortage of men. On the contrary, more volunteers were still coming forward than could be equipped. Parliament and the politicians wanted to give the impression that they were doing something active to aid the war; and conscription seemed the way to do this. Popular clamour insisted that 650,000 'shirkers' lay hidden.... The compulsory call-up proved disappointing. Instead of revealing 650,000 shirkers, it produced a million and a half claims for exemption from men who were performing essential work in industry. Conscription also produced conscientious objectors... bringing home to people for the first time that it was possible to object to the war on high moral grounds. The debate on what the war was about was at last beginning. [32]

Other historians, such as E. S. Turner, have disagreed with Taylor's assessment about the need for conscription. According to Turner:

> By mid-1915...it became increasingly obvious that if Britain was to produce the seventy divisions Kitchner wanted to match allied strengths...a system of compulsion was inevitable. [33]

Both historians agree, however, that once the question of conscription came up, the problem was divisive.

The drive to force men into the military started early. By the summer of 1915, the idea of conscription was current enough to allow at least one recruiting officer to use it as a threat to increase "voluntary" recruitment.[34] Some leaders of the Liberal and Labour parties believed that conscription would cause labor unrest, resentment both at home and in the trenches, and generally make Britain seem little better than Prussianized Germany. Against these sentiments were Lloyd George and his allies in the Liberal Party who wanted conscription, the Conservative Party, the military, and also a popular demand that "something" be done about "shirkers."

Lord Derby, a Conservative who was appointed Director of Recruiting in October 1915, thought he had a compromise in what soon became known as the "Derby scheme." The general outline of the plan was to have all males of service age "attest," that is put his name in the hands of the Government voluntarily, the Government relying on peer pressure and public sentiment for a high turnout. All who attested would then be called up by age [except those in a war-protected job or who already had a personal exemption from before the callup], and all bachelors would be called before married men. The voluntary attesting kept up the illusion of a volunteer army; it was an illusion because if most men did not attest, regular conscription would be substituted. Not surprisingly, the number of those attesting was not high enough to prevent conscription.[35] Lord Derby was forced to conclude:

> [I]t will not be possible to hold married men to
> their attestation unless and until the services of
> single men have been obtained by other means,
> the present system having failed to bring them to
> the colours. [36]

In January 1916, the conscription of single men was introduced,
and universal conscription of men started the following May. For the first
time since the press gangs, it was illegal to avoid fighting for King and
Country. If an unexempted man did not enlist, he was considered a
member of the Reserves, and the authorities quickly went looking for
their new fighting men, who would soon be needed as replacement after
the Battle of the Somme.

> The recruiters who had threatened to 'come and
> fetch' the laggards now made the most of the
> opportunities offered them. In the summer and
> autumn of 1916 something very like the press
> gang was revived in Britain, as police and military
> conducted sudden round-ups at railway stations
> and places of entertainment. [37]

The myth of the unified nation at war was destroyed during early 1916
by the furor over conscription in Great Britain and the uprising in Ireland.
If anything more was needed than these events, and the news from the
fronts in general, to destroy British morale both in the military and on the
home front, it was provided by the news which came out of the British
sector of the Western Front after July 1–the Battle of the Somme.

The Battle of the Somme may have been the most ill-conceived of the many poorly planned offensives which took place on the Western Front. The Somme Offensive changed the way many of the soldiers thought about the War, and this change of attitude, combined with the huge casualty lists, rippled back to the home front.

Although the casualty lists before the Battle of the Somme had often been large, it had still been possible for those at home to believe that life on the Western Front was at least bearable. The 60,000 men killed and wounded in one day made the propaganda about life on the Western Front, such as press reports, rather difficult to believe. The following is Lord Northcliffe's [later in charge of British propaganda] picture of the Western Front soldier:

> I have had little talks with some hundreds of our soldiers during the war, and in regard to care and comfort and nursing, diet and clothes, the provision for reading and smoking, I have never heard a single complaint. The health of all is wonderful. [38]

Although life at the Front was not presented as easy or safe, Northcliffe went to great lengths to show that everything which could be done was being done, and being done well. From the time "Tommy" landed in France until he came home on leave [or came home slightly wounded, given at all times only the finest medical care], he had the best food at all times [not greasy bully beef, beans, tasteless cheese, and stale water], and easy access to anything a wholesome young man could want [no mention, of course, of the separate brothels for enlisted men and officers]. With reports such as those of Northcliffe, it is easy to see why the reports that some of the soldiers were discontented were dismissed as exaggerations.[39]

In short, the home front was no more prepared for the Somme than were the raw conscripts who fought in the later stages of that offensive. Although the casualties of the previous twenty-three months, especially those from the Franco-German battle of Verdun, should have prepared most Britons for what could happen when the army started its major offensive of 1916, few if any were prepared for the ill-planned offensive.[40] There were 20,000 killed and 40,000 wounded on that first day. By the time the offensive ended on November 13, the British had suffered some 420,000 casualties, the French 200,000, and the Germans 450,000. The Allies had advanced about five miles into the German lines over a small section of the entire front.[41]

The nature of the Somme Offensive discouraged those volunteers who were still able to fight and did not bode well for the future of the new conscripts.

> The British were worn down.... Idealism perished on the Somme. The enthusiastic volunteers were enthusiastic no longer. They had lost faith in their cause, in their leaders.... The war ceased to have a purpose.... Rupert Brooke had symbolized the British soldier at the beginning of the war. Now his place was taken by Old Bill, a veteran of 1915, who crouched in a shell crater for want of 'a better 'ole to go to.'... After the Somme men decided the war would go on forever. [42]

This attitude was also reflected on the home front during the winter of 1916-1917.

> ...the general mood...by the end of 1916 was settling into a weary resignation, far from the buoyant optimism of two years earlier. Victory was still certain...but...how, when, and at what cost.... [43]

> 1917 was not so much marked by disillusionment as by discontent. But there was a touch of despair too, as the scale of the terrible bleeding of the war began to seep into the national consciousness: diarists who had once been full of cheery predictions as to the early end of the war are now wondering if it will ever end. [44]

Faced with the twin problems of low morale both on the home front and in the military, the British "establishment"[45] turned once again to propaganda, but the propaganda machines of 1917 were organisms with experience, and a fund of knowledge to draw from. Rather than the high emotions which generated the propaganda of 1914-1915, the new propaganda would try to generate the high emotions themselves.[46]

The new propaganda went two ways, setting both highs and lows. The most famous "low" propaganda was the story of the German Kadaver factories, which was sprung on the breakfasting British people on the morning of April 17, 1917, in a story in the Daily Mail entitled "HUN GHOULS: Oil, Fodder and Dividends From the Dead."

There had been rumors that the Germans had been processing corpses since at least mid-1915. On April 16, however, the Times printed a story from a Berlin paper which mentioned a Kadaverwertunganstalt which rendered oil and pig fodder. Although there were many who correctly realized that the Germans were processing horses and not men, the story was pressed by the Government and believed by many. The story fit in with the old stories of German atrocities: butchered Belgian babies; nuns and priests used as bell clappers; and the first use of poison gas [which was, at least, true]. As Lord Robert Cecil, leader of what can be termed the High Church Tories, said when asked about the corpse factory stories, "In view of the other actions by German military authorities there is nothing incredible in the present charges against them."[47]

Besides the new wave of atrocity propaganda, the apologia of the Somme campaign such as John Masefield's The Old Front Line, patriotic letters from soldiers, like Coninsby Dawson's Carry On, and the like, there also emerged a new type of propaganda after 1916. This new propaganda was not always Government sponsored [especially at first] but built around the themes of a League of All Nations and the concept that the "Great War" should become a "war to end all wars." The Fabian Society pushed the idea of war to end war nearly from the beginning of the Great War, but though a League of Nations Society had been formed in 1915 by a Liberal MP, the idea for what H. G. Wells called a Peace League only gained momentum in 1917. Although the Conservative press was fairly hostile to the idea of a League of Nations or a Peace League [and, it can easily be argued, remained so right through 1939], the fact that President Wilson brought the United States into the Great War espousing, amongst various things, a League, helped carry the idea along. Prominent politicians, including Lloyd George and Lord Robert Cecil, quickly claimed conversion to the idea of aı. international organization as the idea gained popularity for a great variety of reasons.

This change in attitude towards the idea of a League can be seen in a collection of <u>Essays and Addresses in War Time</u> by James, Viscount Bryce, the president of "the British Academy for the promotion of historical, philological, and philosophical studies."[48] The early part of the collection falls neatly into what can be called the "academic defense" of Britain's position and motives in the War.

> Britain stands for the principle of Nationality. She has always given her sympathy to the efforts of a people under a foreign domination to deliver themselves from the stranger and to be ruled by a government of their own.... They [English Liberals] gave that sympathy also to the German movement for national unity form 1848 to 1870, for in those days that movement was led by German Liberals of lofty aims who did not desire, as the recent rulers of Germany have desired, to make their strength a menace to the peace and security of their neighbors. [49]

Bryce's 1916 presidential address to the British Academy dealt with the problems which the War had caused to the concept of international law. In this context, he raised the question of "some kind of federation or league or alliance of nations.[50] Although Bryce stated that "[s]uch ideas cannot be dismissed as visionary,"[51] the general drift of his comments show that he regarded the idea as worthy but probably unworkable. Considering that most of the speech before this point was concerned with showing that war [at least on a small scale] was an often deplorable constant in international affairs, the idea of any international organization, whether a "league, federation, or alliance," as any sort of "peace league" would probably have been regarded as Utopian by Bryce.[52]

The final essay in the collection, "Concerning a Peace League," was written in 1918. Considering the 1916 address, it could be expected that Bryce would argue against the idea of the international organization being primarily a "peace" league, if not against the idea of a league at all. Instead, Bryce argued for a league, but one which conformed to his ideals rather than one where the main purpose was to promote peace. Specifically, Bryce asserts in his opening paragraph, that the idea of a League of Nations could no longer be argued against, and was, in fact, accepted as standard public policy by nearly everyone. Government and independent propaganda had done its job, and people like Bryce were ready to jump on the League bandwagon in order to try to influence what any "league" would be like.

During the winter of 1917-1918, more and more British leaders announced that they favored the idea of a League of Nations. It is difficult to know how seriously these politicians took the idea of some sort of league at this time. As V. H. Rothwell points out,[53] even Lord Robert Cecil, later famous for his connection with the League of Nations and the League of Nations Union,

> remarked that he still thought the only real
> guarantee of future security lay in the defeat of

Germany or in a revolution there. 'The League of Nations may be a buttress to security but it is far too uncertain a project to be relied on as its foundation.' [54]

Thoughts like Cecil's were not, however, for public consumption. In public, the League of Nations was hinted as being the way to insure that there would be no more war. Since concrete proposals were not being discussed [rarely even in private, let alone in public][55] political leaders were able to jump on a bandwagon while not really committing themselves to very much. At the same time, the endorsement of the idea of a League by British leaders allowed Britain [and, to an even greater extent, the United States] to appear to be leading a moral crusade, not just against the Germans [i.e., Prussianism] and the other Central Powers, but against war itself. It also allowed the public the pleasure of being morally superior to the Germans on two counts: not only oppossing the style of war the Germans were said to be using in the "low propaganda," but being totally against war. When the defeat of Germany approached in 1918, the concept of a League of Nations and inter-national justice put forward by President Wilson [along with Wilson's appearance of impartiality and fairness] allowed the German leaders to accept an armistice rather than to try and avert a total German defeat on the battlefield. The Allied propaganda had even worked on the German leaders.

What perceptions could a typical person on the British home front be expected to have remembered out of the mass of unofficial and official propaganda which was dumped on the British public during four years of war? One of the major themes had been that the Germans were barbarians as well as hypocrites. Little wonder that Lloyd George won an election during the first flush of victory on the theme of "Hang the Kaiser" as well as that of "Building Homes Fit For Heroes." Neither should it be unexpected to the historian that later there would be a reaction against the propaganda, turning the Germans into people "just like us."

For the British people, along with those other nations who fought through most of the War, the Great War was a time of sacrifice. Millions of lives had been lost, millions more changed, if not totally ruined. The questions "Has it been worth it?" and "What next?" had been asked during the last months of the War, and although no authoritative voice ever answered, the general answers were, at least at first, "maybe" and "a better life." The British people had been told from the beginning that their cause was just, and much of the propaganda put out was meant to show that position. In addition, for well over a year before the Armistice, the British people had been told that the Great War would be "the war to end war," and that the League of Nations [still, of course, totally undesigned in format or composition] would bring about this new era of peaceful international relations. At the same time, the British had been sacrificing their sons and lovers, as well as their material assets for the War. They were therefore promised "homes fit for heroes" and a new age of prosperity. Those few who doubted these truths, especially the justness of the British cause, were often hounded, sometimes by the Government, other times by individuals, in some cases by mobs.

From 1919 until 1939, the British people were in for a large number of shocks which turned them towards reality. Many of those shocks were economic, and lie outside the scope of this study. All through the interwar period, disillusionment continually built up as unexpected truths came forward. The Government and what would have been called the "establishment" in the 1960s had encouraged illusions about the War and even more about the future peace, mostly to encourage the populace to face the unpleasant short term problems. The people accepted many of these illusions in order to block out the horrors and potential horrors which threatened to engulf them. The political promises made by their Government would never come about. Once the War was over, the British people would learn more about the German side, and even more about what life in the trenches had been like. All those lies, stories, and promises told to the British people by their leaders would be found wanting. What a nation had been taught to be true, and had accepted as true, would be shown to be false. War at first was just, then it was necessary to bring an age of prosperity and peace. The returning soldiers did not get great jobs and nice homes. The War had not brought peace. The British public of the 1930s, raised on the propaganda of the Great War, would be more suspicious of claims of a necessary defense.

NOTES

1. E. S. Turner, Dear Old Blighty [London, 1980], p. 23.

2. Winston S. Churchill, The World Crisis 1911-1914 [New York, 1924], pp. 245-246.

3. Quoted in Turner, p. 33.

4. Malcolm Brown, Tommy Goes to War [London, 1978], p. 17.

5. Arthur Marwick, The Deluge [Boston, 1965], p. 17.

6. For an in depth study of British intellectuals and World War I, see Roland N. Stromberg's Redemption by War [Lawrence, Kansas, 1982]; for the Church of England's role in the Great War, see Albert Marrin's The Last Crusade [Durham, North Carolina, 1974].

7. "The following pages represent the substance of a lecture delivered from notes at University College on 5 October last, and repeated in London and elsewhere from Exeter to Newcastle-on-Tyne." A. F. Pollard, The War: its history and its morals [London, 1915], p. 3.

8. Ibid.

9. Ibid., pp. 5-6.

10. For a fine analysis of those immediate causes of the First World War, see Laurence Lafore's The Long Fuse [Philadelphia, 1971].

11. Pollard, p. 8.

12. Ibid., pp. 9-10. Pollard's statement reflects the attitude of many Englishmen during the earlier stages of the war–war was just another game. This archetypal British attitude is often called the "playing fields of Eton" complex, illustrating the cliche "its not if you win or lose, but how you play the game that counts." The belief that the Germans did not know how to play the game was

well-known. For a slightly later example, the equally archetypal Victorian hero, Sherlock Holmes, told the master German spy he captured on the eve of the War "But you have one quality which is very rare in a German, Mr. Von Bork: you are a sportsman...." Sir Arthur Conan Doyle, "His Last Bow" in The Complete Sherlock Holmes, Volume II [Garden City, New York, 1930], p. 979.

13. Pollard, p. 26.

14. Just a few examples would include works such as Lord Northcliffe's At the War [London, 1916]; J. M. Robertson's War & Civilization [London, 1917]; and George W. E. Russell's The Spirit of England [London, 1915].

15. Both movements were Continental, and claimed few artists of note in Britain, although more than a few students.

16. Stromberg, p. 2.

17. Turner, p. 26.

18. Brown, p. 23. A good selection of propaganda posters from World War I can be found in What Did You Do In The War Daddy [Melbourne, 1983]. The famous poster from which the book gets its title may be found on p. 45.

19. Brooke died of sunstroke according to J. W. Cunliffe, Poems of the Great War [New York, 1916], p. 38, while Robert Wohl states that he died of blood poisoning, The Generation of 1914 [Cambridge, Massachusetts, 1979], p. 90.

20. The closest Brooke ever got to any front was guard duty at Antwerp in October, 1914. Wohl, pp. 89-90.

21. Cunliffe, p. 38. Another good contemporary anthology is A Treasury of War Poetry [Boston, 1916], George Herbert Clarke, ed. Compare Brooke's poem to Rosenberg's "Dead Man's Dump," pp. 109-111 in The Collected Poems of Isaac Rosenberg [London, 1979].

22. "X," War Poems by "X" [London, 1916], p. 64

23. Pierre Nothomb, The Barbarians in Belgium [London, 1915], pp. 124, 126.

24. Ibid., pp. 108-112, 132.

25. Ibid., pp. 23-25.

26. "[F]or a time...conflicts within British society were sublimed by a passionate xenophobia which expressed itself not only in extensive volunteering for the armed forces but also in attacks on aliens. The first months of the war were rife with rumours...in which the sizable German and alien population in Britain came under...suspicion and even attack." John Stevenson, British Society 1914-45 [London, 1984], p. 55.

27. See, for example, the lower photograph opposite p. 51 of John William's The Other Battleground [Chicago, 1972].

28. Stevenson, pp. 55-57, Brown, p. 23.

29. For example, Arnold Toynbee's two volume work on German atrocities, The German Terror in Belgium and The German Terror in France [London, 1917], covers the same material as Barbarians in Belgium, although written two years later.

30. For instance, Hilaire Belloc's two volume work The Elements of the Great War [New York, 1915, volume I, and 1916, volume II], and Lord Ernest Hamilton's The First Seven Divisions [London, 1916].

31. "Italy's entry into the war brought few of the advantages which the Allies had hoped for. The Italian navy...could not be relied on to stop the Austrian submarines.... Economically Italy was a considerable burden.... The Italian army had not recovered from the Libyan War of 1912." A.J.P. Taylor, A History of the First World War [New York, 1963], pp. 55-56. It might also be mentioned that Italy was also a burden to the Allies at the peace conference and to Britain and France throughout most of the interwar period.

32. <u>Ibid</u>., p. 70.

33. Turner, p. 164.

34. <u>Ibid</u>., pp. 162-164.

35. <u>Ibid</u>., p. 165. Marwick gives the figures of 1,150,000 out of 2,179,231 single men [52.78%] attested and 1,152,947 out of 2,832,210 married men [40.71%], p. 78.

36. Marwick, pp. 77-78.

37. Turner, p. 166.

38. Northcliffe, pp. 7-8.

39. For one example, see Dorothy L. Sayers' opinion of her uncle and cousin. James Brabazon, <u>Dorothy L. Sayers</u> [New York, 1982], p. 58.

40. Taylor, pp. 75-79, 82-85.

41. <u>Ibid</u>., pp. 85-86. Taylor's figures are 20,000 killed and 40,000 wounded that first day of battle; Turner's [p. 128] 19,240 and 57,470.

42. Taylor, p. 86.

43. Williams, p. 132.

44. Turner, p. 211.

45. Meaning, in this sense, the British Government, Press, and the self-appointed intellectuals who looked over British interests.

46. Turner, p. 211. Till late 1916 the propaganda machine practically ran under its own steam, churning out a miscellaneous array of slogans, both idealistic and vicious; after 1916 the Government had to deliberately prime the machine by feeding these by-products back into it.

47. <u>Ibid</u>., p. 186. See pages 183-189 for a more complete summary.

48. James, Viscount Bryce, <u>Essays and Addresses in War Time</u> [Freeport, New York, 1968], p. 103.

49. <u>Ibid</u>., pp. 26-27. While there is some truth to Bryce's statement, it is hard to accept Bismarck's policies of the 1860s as part of this "liberal" nationalism.

50. <u>Ibid</u>., p. 135.

51. <u>Ibid</u>.

52. The text runs from pp. 119-140.

53. V. H. Rothwell, <u>British War Aims and Peace Diplomacy 1914-1918</u> [Oxford, 1971], pp. 154-155.

54. Quoted from a letter by Cecil to Balfour, <u>ibid</u>., p. 154.

55. <u>Ibid</u>.

THE WARRIORS' LITERATURE & THE HOME FRONT

Propaganda was the main source of information given to the British home front about the fighting during World War I, and that propaganda was meant to camouflage the true state of affairs at the Western Front.[1] Once the War was over, it was, of course, impossible to keep the worlds of the frontline warriors and of the civilians apart. Those at the Front had tended to know what those at home thought about the War, through letters, newspapers, and the type of propaganda discussed in the first chapter, all of which would be "sent over" by well-meaning friends and relatives. The years 1918-30 were the years in which those at home learned about life at the Front and the attitudes of their "happy warriors." This chapter will examine that learning process in three parts: the first, looking briefly at the nature of the Great War; the second, a study of the general content of the warriors' literature; and last looking at the reaction the British public had to this literature, especially during the years 1928-30.

One of the main reasons why this propaganda was so effective during the First World War was because there really were few other ways, other than propaganda, to hear about the Front at the time. Letters, especially from the ranks, were severely censored and, in addition, those at the Front tended to play down the dangers and conditions. One example of this may be found in Siegfried Sassoon's semi-fictional work Memoirs of an Infantry Officer:

> I had just written a farewell letter to Aunt Evelyn.
> I did not read it through, and I am glad I cannot
> do so now, for it was in the "happy warrior" style
> .... Poor Aunt Evelyn was still comfortingly con-
> vinced that I was transport officer, though I had
> given up that job nearly three months ago. [2]

One reason for this type of letter was to prevent worry at home, another because it was possible to get into trouble with the military authorities if too much information or details were given. A third reason was because most of the soldiers formed what has been called the "us versus them habit."[3] "Us" were the soldiers of the front lines and areas: infantry and artillery, combat officers and their men, British and Empire, Belgians, French, and even the Germans. "Them" were everyone else, in the military or members of family notwithstanding. "Us vs. them" is a recurrent theme in the literature of those who fought in the trenches.

> [Going into battle] was some compensation for the
> loss of last year's day dreams about England
> (which I could no longer indulge in, owing to an
> indefinite hostility to "people at home who couldn't
> understand"). I was beginning to feel rather arro-
> gant toward "people at home." But my mind was
> in a muddle...there was nothing left to believe in
> except "the Battalion spirit." The Battalion spirit
> meant living oneself into comfortable companion-
> ship with the officers and N.C.O.s around one; it
> meant winning the respect, or even the affection,
> of platoon and company. [4]

> [H]e hated the War as much as ever...distrusted
> the motives of the War partisans, and hated the

army. But he liked the soldiers, the War soldiers, not as soldiers but as men.... If the German soldiers were like the men he had seen...that morning, then he liked...them too. He was with them. [5]

[A]s a nation Britain included not only the trench-soldiers themselves and those who had gone home wounded, but the staff, Army Service Corps, lines-of-communication troops, base units, home service units, and all civilians down to the de-tested grades of journalists, profiteers, 'starred' men exempted from enlistment, conscientious objectors, and members of the Government. [6]

The atmosphere of the home front was one which made "patriotism righteous."[7] The British cause was considered just [defending "Little Belgium" and going to the aid of "valiant France" during the early years, fighting a "war to end war" in the last year or so] and the public was assured that their sons and lovers were happy and well cared for.[8] Life for the British soldier in the trenches in France, however, gave rise to other opinions.

While historians will always argue both sides of the question of whether or not a major war between the two alliance systems of Europe had to be fought at some time and in some manner in the first quarter century of the twentieth century, there can be little if any doubt, however, that the way in which World War I was fought on the Western Front from late 1914 through early 1918 was the most unthinking, unproductive, and wasteful manner in which war has ever been fought by both sides of a conflict. Over the course of more than three years, millions of men, sometimes over 100,000 at a time, were hurled against machine guns, barbed wire, mines, and defensive trenches manned by nearly equal numbers–while at the same time being shelled by high explosives and at times poison gas–until there were no more men who could be thrown in while still being able to hold the original line. Between this slaughter the great barrages of deafening artillery and mortar fire could start up at any minute [usually to prepare for, or defend against, an attack]. There was also the ever-present danger of sniper fire, machine gun sweeps, probing raids, and wiring parties into no man's land. Such were the bare bones of life in the trenches, along with poor food, sodden trenches [especially in the British sector], rats, and, in areas where there had been an offensive, large numbers of unburied bodies. Life in the trenches can best be summed up by a title of one of the popular histories on the subject: <u>Eye-deep in Hell</u>.[9] As horrible as many of the scenes are in the poetry, memoirs, and fiction written by the warriors themselves, they often pale beside the reality presented by some of the secondary works.[10] Although it is impossible to go into great detail in this work, it must be made clear that many of the incidents which shocked the British public in the 1920s when they first appeared in the literature are borne out in the secondary material available. In fact, the literature is only more powerful because of the personal narrative.

For the British soldier on the Western Front, the War was divided into two parts: before and after the Somme Offensive. At first glance, this change of attitude is remarkable. The British army was much larger in late 1916 then it had been the year before, and so was able to occupy a larger area of the front. These new areas were, for the most part, "healthier;" that is, they were entrenched in chalk rather than in Flanders mud. The nature of trench life remained basically the same, although some rations were cut in 1917 and 1918.[11] The nature of the offensives also remained much the same from late 1914 until the German breakthrough in early 1918. Three things effected this change of attitude, and although only one was directly linked to the nature of the Somme Offensive, the three came together at the same time and reinforced each other.

In 1914 and early 1915, the British army had been the only totally professional army on the field. The troops were professionals or members of the home reserve units known as the Territorials, as opposed to the largely conscripted armies of the other armies.[12] This makeup had started to change by the battle of Loos, and by the start of the Somme Offensive [July 1, 1916] the British army was made up of volunteers with various amounts of training, lightly seasons with experienced regular troops. The volunteers were men who, before August 1914, had probably never thought about joining the army. They enlisted out of love of country, idealism, and family or peer pressure, but unlike most of the soldiers of the other countries, they had all signed up more or less as volunteers. It was these men who attached the German trenches at the walking pace ordered by their commanding officers; it was these once enthusiastic volunteers who made up the majority of the 30,000 killed and wounded that first hour of the attack,[13] the 20,000 killed that first day,[14] the 420,000 killed and wounded by the time the Offensive ended in mid-November.[15] It was also these men who wrote the majority of what I have termed the warriors' literature, rather than the regulars who preceded them or the conscripts who came after them.

While the changeover in mid-War from a professional and volunteer army to a conscript army had its effect on morale, along with the fact that there seemed no end to the War in sight, the Somme Offensive itself seems to have the main factor in the loss of British morale. As A. J. P. Taylor put it:

> The British were worn down.... Idealism perished on the Somme. The enthusiastic volunteers were enthusiastic no longer. They had lost faith in their cause, in their leaders, in everything except loyalty to their fighting comrades. The war ceased to have a purpose. It went on for its own sake, as a contest of endurance. [16]

Or, as a later historian put it succinctly, "[p]opular support [for the war] was blunted naturally enough by the carnage of 1914-16...."[17]

While the Somme Offensive may have been the main cause for the loss of British morale, the changing nature of the army was a major factor as well. Where the professional and volunteer army had often been recruited from the same geographical and social areas [the most famous examples in the volunteer army being the numerous "Pal" units[18]], the old units were filled after mid-July 1916 by conscripts from all over the United Kingdom. The peer group pressure which had helped to keep morale up [and which may have caused many to enlist in the first place] was gone, and many soldiers also had to face the loss of pre-War as well as wartime friends, not just from death, but because wounded were not returned to their old units as had been the case before the Somme Offensive. The new conscripts were not only those who had been too young to join up, but also older men who had avoided volunteering in the first place, and who were often considered shirkers by the volunteers. On top of everything else, while officers got leave every three to eight months, privates were lucky to get ten days a year.[19] As the months dragged on, the minor conflicts natural between men thrown together under difficult circumstances would magnify themselves.

Finally, the Somme Offensive helped break the British spirit both in the field and at home because the huge losses were in vain. Had the British pushed the Germans back a fair distance, or had they achieved the ever-awaited breakthrough, their morale may have held despite the heavy losses. Instead, the troops who survived had to live through another winter in the open trenches and looked forward to another offensive in the spring, with little confidence in their high command. When the next offensive finally came, it proved most of the fears of the troops correct. Passchendaele [or third Ypres] was in many ways a re-peat of the Somme, although with fewer casualties–the British lost 300,000 killed and wounded rather than 420,000.[20] When the 1917 offensive failed, like those of 1915 and 1916, the survivors once more had to look towards another winter in the trenches–the worst winter of the War as it turned out–and at least another year of battle. Is it little wonder that between the winters of 1916-17 and 1917-18 the troops began to wonder if the War would ever end?[21] For many, like Sassoon, it may have became a matter of mental rather than physical survival:

> Having ceased to wonder when the War would
> be over, I couldn't imagine myself anywhere else
> but on active service, and I was no longer able to
> indulge in reveries about being at home.... I
> suppose this meant that I was making a forced
> effort to keep going to the end. [22]

In short, the patriotic army which had fought the offensives of Loos and the Somme was destroyed in spirit as well as in body by these offensives, by the conditions, and by the seeming endlessness of the War. It was these men who wrote the best war poetry, and these men whose memoirs would change the tone of British opinion about the War. Their views were the more powerful, not because their work formed the majority of the works which had the War as a main theme, or even because their view was the only reasonable one possible,[23] but because their view of the War, from the trenches, was so widely shared by the men who had fought alongside them. Together, they formed a solid group in the general population, and there was an even larger number of people who wanted, or needed, to learn the "truth about the war," and who would look to these warriors rather than their military leaders, who were often nearly as far away from the fighting as the political leaders, for this truth.[24]

The warriors' literature took many forms: memoirs; poetry; plays; novels. Some of the works, especially the best poetry,[25] were written during the War. Some of the other works were started immediately after the War, but most of the non-poetic works were products of years of reflection.[26] Although the variety of forms may be of interest to the literary historian or critic, and the causes for delayed publication of concern to the psychohistorian and biographer, the content is the main interest for the social and intellectual historian. The content of the warriors' literature is fairly consistent in the themes expounded. Some of the major themes will be shown below, illustrated with examples from some of the works. One of the primary ideas, the dislike of "them," was illustrated above, along with the minor theme of keeping those at home from worrying.

Unsurprisingly, one of the main themes of the literature was the horrors and terrors of life in the trenches and during attacks. Some of the poems which pertain to this topic include Isaac Rosenberg's "Dead Man's Dump," Herbert Read's "Kneeshaw goes to War," and "Attack" by Siegfried Sassoon.[27] The prose, however, contains just as graphic pictures of life in France as the poetry.

> [M]y own unwelcome but persistent retrospect was the shell-hole there in a captured trench used by us as a latrine, with those two flattened German bodies in it, tallowfaced and dirty-stubble, one spectacled, with fingers hooking the handle of a bomb; and others had much worse to remember. [28]

> After the first day or two the corpses swelled and stank.... Those we could not get in from the German wire continued to swell until the wall of the stomach collapsed, either naturally or when punctured by a bullet; a disgusting smell would float across. The colour of the dead faces changed

from white to yellow-grey, to red, to purple, to
green, to black, to slimy. [29]

There was, of course, much more to the horrors of war and of life
at the Front than the huge number of decaying corpses and the larger
number of rats which fed on them.[30] Stories of the effects of shelling
occur in most of the works, as do the tales of the fear the writers felt
when they had to carry out probing raids, wiring parties, and patrols,[31]
or when they had to wait for an enemy attack. [This last event can best
be seen in Richard Aldington's novelette, At All Costs.[32]]

As mentioned above, shellings were common at the Front, and the
men had no choice but to endure them as best they could.

> The gods were thundering. At times the sound
> dwarfed me into such infinitesimal littleness that a
> feeling of security was endangered....
> The cannonade raged for three hours.... [33]

The effects of such "cannonades" were more than just destruction, and
the men had to live with these effects as well as the shelling. After one
shelling, the soldiers had to rescue their rations, since the ration party
had been killed by the bombardment.

> "Where's the bread, Bill?" I asked.
> "In that there sandbag,..."
> I opened the bag and brought out the load. It
> felt very moist. I looked at it and saw that it was
> coloured dark red....

We were very hungry, and hungry men are not fastidious.
We made a good meal.
When we had eaten we went out and buried the dead. [34]

The horrors of life at the front, combined with all the other circumstances described above and below, helped elevate the soldiers into a frenzy when they finally got into battle, and nearly every work contains many passages which show this. It led Sassoon, for example, into activity that gained him the nickname of "Mad Jack," and may account, at least in part, for the following actions.

When we were at Messines they [German bodies] lay about thick. I pulled the teeth out of one of them and made a necklace of them.

[W]e took a lot of prisoners in those trenches yesterday morning.... [An officer] got one hand above his head, and a pair of field-glasses in the other. He held the glasses out to S——... and said, "Here you are sergeant, I surrender." S—— said, "Thank you, sir," and took the glasses with his left hand. At the same moment, he tucked the butt of his rifle under his arm and shot the officer straight through the head....
It wasn't only him. Another did exactly the same thing.

M'Crone's mother never sends her son any money lest he gets into the evil habit of smoking cigarettes. He is of a religious turn of mind and delights in singing hymns.... I never head him swear before, but at Loos his language would make a navvy...green with envy.... [N]ow, inflicting pain on others, he was a fiend personified; such transformations are common occurrences on the field of honour.

Through these days of battle one lived in an elevated state of mind which a doctor might have defined as neurosis. The strange sense of dual personality which comes to so many people at moments of high tension was hardly ever absent. There as an arguing realism, a cynical side to one's nature that...suggested dangers, and against it there strove a romantic ardour for the battle that was almost joyful. While the mind took sides...the body seemed numb and void. An emptiness almost like a physical pain tormented my bowels.... Our duty somehow done, we returned to camp at midnight. Next day I was miserable beyond belief, description or cure. A sort of insensible numbness, such as seems to envelop criminals in the condemned cell, settled on my spirits.... [35]

This is not to claim that the actions and reactions of the soldiers were in any way unusual for soldiers in any war, before or after World War I. It may even be possible that they were very typical. They were not, however, the reactions and actions which those at home were led to expect from their sons and lovers. Each and every one of the above quotations could have stirred up the reaction which will be made described in the last section of this chapter: that those who stayed at home revolted against the realism which the war novels and memoirs showed. Before that reaction is described, however, the rest of the soldiers' views must be presented.

The opposing side to the horrors of the battlefield and trenches for the front line soldier was the tedium which occupied most of his time. Fortunately for the sanity of the men, very little time was spent under fire out of their total time of service. Charles Carrington figured that he spent 1916 in the following manner:

> 65 days in the front lines
> 36 "   in support positions [and under fire]
> 120 "   in reserve
> 73 "   rest leave in France with his men
> 21 "   in hospital [with German measles]
> 10 "   leave in Britain
> 9 "   at regimental base camp
> 14 "   travel [36]

Of course, of the 65 days Carrington spent in the front lines, 13 straight were spent in the midst of the Somme offensive, where he and his men captured and held a German trench under very difficult conditions. Those of his men who survived were spent with him on "rest leave."[37]

Some of the time which soldiers spent in reserve or at the "rest camps" might be what was called "free time":

> During the off days, we killed time as best we
> could, gaining our first experience of the greatest
> bane of the life of a soldier, boredom, cafard, or
> whatever you call it. [38]

Most of the time the soldiers had in reserve, however, was at least organized so as to prevent lethargy:

>   Reserve did not spell rest.   We were over-
> whelmed with working parties.   One day was
> spent in the support lines at Hannescamps...eight
> hours digging, ten miles' marching; the next on a
> strong-point four miles westward....   In the inter-
> vals there were the inevitable kit inspections...foot
> inspections, gasmask inspections, guards, minor
> fatigues.... [39]

Time spent in the rest camps during the summer of 1916 could be short, as Carrington found out.

> Twice already we had gone into the Battle of the
> Somme to make food for powder, and now a se-
> cond time [i.e., after having fought 13 straight
> days–their second tour of duty at the front during
> the Somme Offensive] were withdrawn for rest and
> training, and to be made 'up to strength' by drafts
> of new recruits sent out from England.   A dis-
> banded battalion of cyclists from East Anglia gave
> us one of the best drafts...sufficient in numbers for
> us to be able to undertake a third tour in the battle
> late in August. [40]

Officers often had to improvise "busy work" in order to keep up their men's spirits.   Life on the line and in support may have been "tedious and repetitional"[41] and may have deserved the epitaph of "the clogging monopoly,"[42]   but at least it had a set routine when not disturbed by attacks and counterattacks. It was life between tours of duty which challenged officers and men alike.

> Meanwhile we were in what was called "Corps Reserve," and Colonel Easby had issued the order "carry on with platoon training" (a pronouncement which left us free to kill time as best we could).... It was difficult to know what to do with my bored and apathetic platoon.
> I wasn't a competent instructor, and my sergeant was conscientious but unenterprising. Infantry Training, which was the only manual...had been written years before trench-warfare "came into its own"...and the...practical Handbook for the Training of Platoons was not issued until nearly twelve months afterwards. [43]

Sassoon [the officer quoted above] solved his problem with various types of physical training,[44] but an unanswerable question remains: how many other officers did not solve the problem?

The above subject naturally leads to the problem of mental fatigue on the lines, a contributing factor of what was then simply called "shell-shock" as well as what has now been identified as "delayed stress syndrome." The problem of shell-shock occurred in all ranks in the front line and support troops, but may have affected the lower ranks the worst.

> Mud and boredom and discomfort seemed to take the guts out of them. If an officer crumpled up, Kinjack sent him home as useless...and most of them ended up with safe jobs in England. But if a man became a dud in the ranks, he just remained where he was until he was killed or

wounded .... I could never understand how they
managed to keep as cheery as they did through
such drudgery and discomfort, with nothing to
look forward to.... [45]

Signs of nervous fatigue are very common in the warriors'
literature, but many of the accounts follow the symptoms put forth below.

Being young and strong, I stood the physical conditions pretty well, and generally recovered from
the effects of trench life after a night's sleep. On
the other hand, the shell-fire began to tell on me.
The terrors of battle added to the hardships of arc-
tic exploration were overwhelming, and after three
tours in the front of the Butte I was a nervous
wreck. Nor, I suppose, was I alone in this, as
one-third of the whole division went sick.... [46]

Finally, many of the soldiers affected by nervous fatigue [being
windy] would fall victim to one of the various forms of shell-shock, a term
which could cover anything from the reason a soldier would commit
suicide in the trenches,[47] to general uselessness, to violence.

Having now been in the trenches for five months,
I had passed my prime....
Between three weeks and four weeks he [an
officer] was at his best, unless he happened to
have any particular bad shock or sequence of
shocks. Then his usefulness gradually declined
as neurasthenia developed. At six months he was
still more or less all right; but by nine or ten
months, unless he had been given a few weeks'

> rest...he usually became a drag on the other
> company officers. After a year or fifteen months
> he was often worse than useless....
>
> Officers had a less laborious but a more nervous
> time than the men. There were proportionately
> twice as many neurasthenic cases among officers
> as among men. [48]

Perhaps, as Graves pointed out, the officers had a "more nervous time than the men," but it is just as likely that the men's problems were more often overlooked by the higher military authorities "until he was killed or wounded," as Sassoon pointed out in the quote above.

The last stage of shell-shock [or neurasthenia] could be nightmares, such as those of Sassoon.

> More than once I wasn't sure whether I was awake
> or asleep; the war was half shadow and half
> sinking firelight.... Shapes of mutilated soldiers
> came crawling across the floor; the floor seemed
> to be littered with fragments of mangled flesh.
> Faces glared upward; hands clutched at neck or
> belly; a livid grinning face with bristly moustache
> peered at me above the edge of my bed; his
> hands clawed at the sheets. [49]

Amazingly enough it was not dreams like the above which landed Sassoon in a mental ward [the dream above occurred before Sassoon was sent to the mental hospital], but his own one man campaign to stop the War.[50]

While the physical scars carried back to Britain were often obvious,[51] the mental scars were not. How many men kept the habits of the War like Robert Graves?

> I would find myself working out tactical problems, planning how best to hold the Upper Artoo valley against an attack from the sea, or where to place a Lewis gun if I were to rush Dolwreiddiog Farm from the brow of the hill, and what would be the best cover for my rifle-grenade section. I still had the Army habit of commandeering anything of uncertain ownership...also a difficulty in telling the truth.... [52]

How many men had nightmares like Sassoon, long after the War ended? How many ended their days in mental hospitals like Ivor Gurney?[53] How many women suffered from the knowledge which was not kept from them during the War, like Vera Brittain? The number cannot be known, but for most of the people involved, the catharsis of the memoir was never invoked, and any outlet is a metter of speculation.[54] In any case, the returning men had to integrate into a society which they had despised for up to four years. They were promised "homes fit for heroes," jobs, and hope. They found unemployment and public apathy once the cheering stopped.[55] Britain had to make the peace as well as celebrate the victory, and worried more about converting from a wartime economy rather than converting the warriors. Interwar British economic history is the story of recession and depression, with only occasional periods of prosperity.[56]

"Apathy" bests describes the public attitude toward the First World War between 1920 and 1927, but this attitude would change. Evidence of this change can be seen in The Novels of World War I: An Annotated Bibliography,[57] which has traced many of the novels about the War [not just the warriors' literature] which appeared in English between 1914 and mid-1980. The two peaks of fictional output are 1918-1919 and 1930:

1914	9	1928	20
1915	42	1929	38
1916	60	1930	57
1917	73	1931	17
1918	117	1932	24
1919	112	1933	8
1920	33	1934	10
1921	14	1935	13
1922	15	1936	14
1923	7	1937	13
1924	8	1938	7
1925	9	1939	6
1926	12	1940-	
1927	16	1980	141

The novels of the period 1928-30 include the first two segments of Sassoon's trilogy; Aldington's Death of a Hero and Roads to Glory; and the novelization of the 1929 stage hit Journey's End by R. C. Sherriff; as well as the English version of Remarque's All Quiet on the Western Front and, from the USA, Hemingway's A Farewell to Arms. Perhaps of more importance than the novels were the memoirs. The period 1928-30 included Blunden's Undertones of War, perhaps the most important of the works; Graves' Good-bye to All that; Carrington's A Subaltern's War; Chapman's A Passionate Prodigality; and Herbert Read's Ambush.

Except for the poetry [for the most part was written and collected before 1923] the works about the War during the period 1919-27 tended to be romance and adventure stories which happened to take place during the War;[58] novels which used the War as a backdrop or explanation for motives; regimental histories;[59] and the biographies and memoirs of the generals. Compared to the vastness of this other work, the poetry could be explained away as Wartime exaggeration. The post-1927 warriors' literature changed that.

Robert Wohl, in his The Generation of 1914, suggests that the legend of the "Lost Generation" in Britain [lost in the sense of killed as well as the more American sense of cut off from other generations] occurred not because of the high losses the British suffered [the Germans and French lost both higher numbers and higher percentages], but because of the high losses of the public school and University junior officers.

> Most of them were killed on the battlefields of Gallipoli, Ypres, Loos, the Somme, Passchendaele, and Cambrai. Those who were not killed were mutilated in mind and body. They limped home in 1919 to find that their sacrifice had been in vain.... Youth had been defeated by age.... Few in number, tired and shell-shocked, disillusioned by what they found at home, they sat helplessly...and watched the old politicians...squander their victory. [60]

This is a very fair version of the attitudes presented by the warriors' literature. Wohl basically agrees, however, with Douglas Jerrold's book The Lie About the War, which argued, in the late 1920s, that the warriors' literature then coming out was misleading because it represented only a small percentage of the attitudes towards the War.

> These lonely and uninfluential voices [such as Jerrold's] failed, however, to dissuade the majority of the English literary establishment from what had not become an idée fixe. [61]

Wohl puts the blame for this on the junior officer class, whose world was changed between 1914 and 1919 [but not, in reality, just because of the War]. They had lost a higher percentage of their fellows during the War. For example, of the 5,588 Old Etonians who served, 1,159 [20.7%] were killed.[62] Wohl is perfectly correct in pointing out that even amongst this class of men, most who went came back,[63] in calling the myth "elitist nonsense,"[64] and pointing out that in many ways the "myth of the missing generation" "became a means of accounting for the failures of the present" and "reflected the natural guilt of the survivors who knew they had no right to live when those around them had died."[65] Wohl misses the point that Britain was, and still is to a great extent, a very elitist country. While the term "missing generation" does mainly mean, as Wohl points out, "missing elite,"[66] the term meant more than just

> the decimation, partial destruction, and psycho-
> logical disorientation of the graduates of public
> schools and universities who had ruled England
> during the previous half century. [67]

In a nation as class oriented, and with an educational system as poor as, turn-of-the-century Britain, this missing elite could very well have ruled for the next half century. It is very easy for Wohl to point out that both Eden and Macmillan, who were from this generation, became Prime Minister[68] [Wohl left Attlee off the list for some reason—as well as the fact that Churchill also served a few months on the Western Front], but it appeared that members of the War generation had very little power in the 1930s, when the missing generation was said to be missing from politics. Attlee only became leader of the Labour Party because so many of the other [older] leaders had been defeated in the 1931 general election, and his position was not really secure at any time [although it was rarely as insecure as was sometimes thought]. Three of the youngest men in Chamberlain's cabinet [including Eden] were forced out in 1938 because of disagreements over foreign policy, taking junior ministers also from the war generation with them. The average age of Chamberlain's first War Cabinet was well over 60. In an era which often concentrated on youth, the apparent lack of young national political leaders was something to remark on, even if not remarkable.

Wohl's arguments against the world-view and view of the War which the surviving elite fashioned for themselves are only academic. The decimation of an elite was thought to have hurried on "unfavorable" [by members of the upper class] social and political changes, and even if today's historians and social scientists believe that these changes would have occurred in some form in any event, that view won general acceptance, and must be dealt with.

The best of the early analyses of the warriors' literature and its relation to general British society is found in A. C. Ward's The Nineteen-Twenties: Literature and Ideas in the Post-war Decade [1930] in the chapter entitled "The Unhappy Warriors."[69] As a "warrior" himself, Ward understood the conflicts between "us" and "them." Ward took the time to counter Jerrod by explaining why the warriors' literature contained a valid point of view, and pointing out to all concerned that it was not the only point of view which should be presented to the reading public.

Ward also presents, and destroys, the case for attacking the "lie about the war," showing that the lies did not come from the warriors.

> The aggressive civilians' view of war is...important, since it counts for so much in the formation of public opinion about war. British soldiers have won a war; they want to believe that it has been won by an army of gentlemen in a gentlemanly way. Only when war is wrapped in a haze of romantic illusion has the British public sufficient moral courage to contemplate war.... The soldiers, too, must be romanticized and sentimentalized.

> [F]acts hurt the public conscience so badly that attempts are made to salve the hurt by declaring that the facts are not as stated; or that the publication of those facts is a libel...whereas it is...no more than the record of what happened to certain individual men. [70]

Ward goes on to ask the "aggressive civilians" which they would have preferred: the soldiers to have remained morally pure [as, it will be remembered, they were portrayed in the propaganda] or to have lost the War?[71]

In the end, however, the critics' complaints against the warriors' literature were drowned out by a rising tide of disillusionment, as the illusions brought about by the propaganda were destroyed by the realities of the new literature about the War.[72] This disillusionment was caught up in and reinforced by the reaction to the overall postwar world. As Wohl puts it, "What survivors found upon returning was not a home fit for heroes, but a 'long weekend' in which life was...'downhill all the way' and 'a contrary experience.'"[73] The men from the trenches were tired and disillusioned, and so were many other people in Britain, and the literature about the War from those who had served in the trenches helped bring about that state.

The 1920s were in general a time when illusions were being stripped away, a time when "the strange death of liberal England"[74] was being acknowledged by many, along with the certain death of the late Victorian/Edwardian social order. The warriors' literature took away the illusion of a united country making glorious sacrifices for a just and noble cause. The realistic war literature took away the glory of those sacrifices and showed the gore which took the place of that glory. The warriors' literature showed the real price—the horrors and terror which the young men of Europe paid for the dream of a better world and the realities of power politics. Those on the home front had known the discomforts of rationing and the shock of the telegram, now they knew that there was a cost to the men who fought besides that of life and limb. Postwar life was enough to show that the Great War had not brought about a better world, and that what the British public had been taught to accept about the aims of the War were lies. The warriors' literature showed that what the public had been told about how the War had been fought was also a lie, and, most importantly, this literature insured that the British public, and their leaders, knew and would not forget the price of fighting a modern war.

NOTES

1. For just one example of this type of propaganda, see Lord Northcliffe's <u>At the War</u> [London, 1916], especially pp. 7-8.

2. While written as fiction, <u>Memoirs of a Fox-Hunting Man</u>, <u>Memoirs of an Infantry Officer</u>, and <u>Sherston's Progress</u> are mainly fictional in the sense that the names have been changed and minor details rearranged. The Sherston trilogy is usually found separate, but cited here is <u>The Complete Memoirs of George Sherston</u> [London, 1937]. The page number will be proceeded by the initials of the original work. [MFM, MIO, SP]. MIO, p. 301.

3. Paul Fussell, <u>The Great War and Modern Memory</u> [London, 1975], p. 79-90; Bernard Bergonzi, <u>Heroes' Twilight</u> [London, 1965], p. 61; C. Day Lewis, <u>The Collected Poems of Wilfred Owen</u> [London, 1964], p. 22. In most, if not all, of the cases presented in this chapter, many more examples could have been culled just from the small selection of literature selected for use. Dozens more works could have been used, and hundreds more examples could have easily been cited. Space and the sanity of both reader and author have dictated this more limited approach.

4. MIO, pp. 420-421.

5. Richard Aldington, <u>Death of a Hero</u> [Garden City, New York, 1929], p. 268. Patrick MacGill, <u>The Great Push</u> [Dover, New Hampshire, 1984], p. 229; and "Charles Edmonds" [Charles Edmund Carrington], <u>A Subaltern's War</u> [New York, 1972], p. 188, both echo Aldington's point.

6. Robert Graves, <u>Good-bye to All That</u> [Garden City, New York, 1957], p. 188. See also Julian Grenfell's poem "Prayer for those on the Staff," Bergonzi, pp. 48-49; Carrington, pp. 64-65; Guy Chapman, <u>A Passionate Prodigality</u> [New York, 1966], pp. 13, 15, 58-59, 85, 104-105, 138-139, 206-207; and Billy Congreve, <u>Armageddon Road</u> [London, 1982], p. 13. For a different

perspective, see Alfredo Bonadeo's Mark of the Beast [Lexington, Kentucky, 1989].

7. Turner, p. 26.

8. For example, see the "Sketches from Tommy's Life" in Brown, pp. 47-49.

9. John Ellis, Eye-deep in Hell [New York, 1976]. Other titles which could fit just as well would be A. Stuart Dolden's memoirs, Cannon Fodder [Poole, Dorset, 1980] or Bonadeo's Mark of the Beast. Some writers, as Bonadeo points out, have gone so far as to call the fighting on the Western Front and some other areas as the concentration camps of the Great War. Bonadeo, pp. 101-102.

10. Besides the works of Ellis and Brown, cited above, the other general work about life in the trenches which has been used is Alan Lloyd's The War in the Trenches [New York, 1976].

11. It should be pointed out, however, that the Germans suffered more than the Allies did from shortness of supplies, especially after the winter of 1916-1917. Ellis, pp. 127-128.

12. For a good oral history survey of these men, see Lyn Macdonald's 1914. [New York, 1988].

13. Martin Middlebrooke, The First Day on the Somme [New York, 1972], p. 129.

14. Ibid., p. 244.

15. A. J. P. Taylor, A History of the First World War [New York, 1963], p. 86.

16. Ibid. The best three books on the Somme from the British point of view are Middlebrooke's classic, cited above, Lyn Macdonald's oral history Somme [London, 1983] and Terry Norman's The Hell They Call High Wood [London, 1984]. Among the many references in the warriors' literature, see especially Carrington, pp. 113, 120.

17. Richard S. Thompson, The Atlantic Archipelago [Lewiston, NY, 1986], p. 350.

18. Patrick MacGill, for one example, served in the London Irish, and there are many other examples. For a short essay on the "pals" and "chums" units, see Brown, pp. 34-37.

19. Ellis, p. 157. Brown records one case where the man only received leave after 16 months on p. 224. Officers and sergeants were also sent to schools more often than were the lower ranks, and usually these "schools" amounted to rest camps by the end of the war. See also MIO, p. 310.

20. Taylor, p. 123. The losses of July 1 represented about 14% of the total British casualties for the five month Somme offensive. For an account of Passchendaele, see Edwin Campion Vaughan's diary, Some Desperate Glory [New York, 1988], pp. 181-232.

21. See the Bruce Bairnsfather cartoon reproduced in Brown, p. 126, captioned 'A.D. Nineteen Fifty, "I see the War Babies Battalion is a coming out."' See also Carrington, p. 113, and MacGill, p. 124.

22. SP, p. 646. Also see Carrington, p. 186.

23. The views of World War I presented by the generals, staff, support troops, those on the homefront, etc., in their memoirs and fiction were just as valid views of their experiences of the war, but became dominated by the works of the front line troops.

24. For a combination of near Front Line experiences and the effects of losses caused by the war, the best work is Vera Brittain's Testament of Youth [New York, 1970].

25. Some of the books which came out in Britain during the war were Robert Graves' Over the Brazier [1916] and Fairies and Fusiliers [1917]; Siegfried Sassoon's The Old Huntsman [1917] and Counter-Attack [1918]; and Severn and Somme by Ivor Gurney [1917].

26. For example, Graves' work Goodbye to All That started off as a novel in 1916 [Graves, p. 91] and Carrington's A Subaltern's War was first written in 1919-20 [Carrington, p. 7] mostly on the boat trip to New York during the summer vacation of 1920 [Carrington, letter to author, May 29, 1985], and Aldington started Death of a

Hero during the winter of 1918-19, but did not finish and revise it until 1928.

27. Rosenberg, pp. 109-111; Herbert Read, Collected Poems of Herbert Read [London, 1966], pp. 154-155; Siegfried Sassoon, Collected Poems 1908-1956 [London, 1956], p. 71.

28. Edmund Blunden, Undertones of War [London, 1928], pp. 112-113.

29. Graves, p. 128; see also. p. 114.

30. See Vaughn, p. 134, and the poem "Living Sepulchers" by Richard Aldington, in The Complete Poems of Richard Aldington [London, 1948], p. 86. The references to rats in the literature are far too numerous to begin citation, as are the references to lice. For one, see "The Immortals" by Rosenberg, Rosenberg, pp. 107-108.

31. For one such patrol story, see SP, pp. 645-650.

32. Richard Aldington, At All Costs [London, 1930]. This novelette first appeared in Aldington's collection Road to Glory.

33. MacGill, pp. 161-162.

34. Ibid., pp. 204-205.

35. The first quote is from Carrington, p. 53; the second is from Chapman, p. 99; the third is from MacGill, pp. 84-85 [see also Vaughn, pp. 141-147]; the fourth is from Carrington again, p. 35; while the final quote is ibid., p. 132. See also the story of Julian Grenfell in John Press' Poets of World War I [Windsor, 1983], p. 14.

36. Carrington, p. 120.

37. Ibid., pp. 62-105. The number of men surviving could be very small. Out of the 90 men in Vaughn's 'D' company who started the battle of Passchendaele, fifteen were alive twelve days later. Vaughn, p. 232.

38. Chapman, p. 25.

39. <u>Ibid</u>., p. 46.

40. Carrington, pp. 114-115.

41. MIO, p. 407.

42. <u>Ibid</u>., p. 309.

43. <u>Ibid</u>., p. 409.

44. <u>Ibid</u>., pp. 409-410.

45. <u>Ibid</u>., pp. 310-311.

46. Carrington, p. 118.

47. Graves, p. 103.

48. <u>Ibid</u>., pp. 171-172. At times, "windy" seems to be Edwin Vaughn's favorite adverb, adjective, and verb.

49. MIO, pp. 453-454. For experiences in mental ward and around "mental" patients, see SP pp. 517-551 and Graves pp. 252-254. There was a new play off Broadway based on the meeting in a mental hospital between two of the greatest war poets, Sassoon and Owen, entitled <u>Not About Heroes</u> during the autumn of 1985, showing the continued interest in this material.

50. MIO, pp. 454-514. For Graves' version, Graves, pp. 260-264.

51. The young men arriving at the Oxford train station during the early 1920s and being nearly surrounded by handicapped veterans in the 1980 movie "Chariots of Fire" is but one example of the physical scars remaining in the collective British memory.

52. Graves, p. 287.

53. Although, in Gurney's case, it must be remembered that his psychological problems were in evidence before the war, although they did not become crippling until the early 1920s.

54. The British passion for mysteries during the interwar period may have been one such outlet.

55. For an early example of the trouble involved in getting demobilized and in getting a job, see Chapman, pp. 274-281.

56. The four best sources for interwar British social history are Charles Loch Mowat's Britain Between the Wars, A.J.P. Taylor's English History 1914-1945, John Stevenson's British Society 1914-45, and, almost a primary source, Robert Graves and Alan Hodges' The Long Week-End.

57. Philip E. Hager and Desmond Taylor, The Novels of World War I [New York, 1981].

58. Most of the novels listed in The Novels of World War I fall into this general category, and added, for the uninformed, to the romance of the war.

59. Carrington, who wrote a realistic war memoir, also wrote the history of his regiment [War Record, 1922].

60. Ibid., p. 85.

61. Ibid., p. 109. Wohl includes Carrington amongst those voices, and cites complaints Carrington made in later years [reflected in Carrington's calling his work "sentimental" in his letter to me; at the same time he suggests this attitude is because of the length of time and changes in himself since it was written]. While it is true Carrington wishes to distance himself from the strident voices of Sherriff, Blunden, etc., the great use made of Carrington's work in this chapter suggests he did not succeed.

62. Wohl, p. 115.

63. Ibid., It must be remembered, as Wohl does not, that the point was as much what the soldiers had to go through as well as the relative percentages of total population lost.

64. Ibid., p. 113.

65. Ibid., p. 115.

66. Ibid., p. 120.

67. _Ibid._, pp. 120-121.

68. _Ibid._, p. 115.

69. A. C. Ward, _The Nineteen-Twenties_ [London, 1930], pp. 141-142. Ward's review of Jerrod is on pp. 146-149, and this chapter covers pp. 140-167.

70. Ward, pp. 143, 145.

71. _Ibid._, p. 145. Early bibliographic references to editorials both for and against the warriors' point of view are easily found throughout Ward's chapter.

72. "By the end of the 1920s most English intellectuals believed that the war had been a general and unmitigated disaster, that England's victory was in reality a defeat, and hence that the men who had caused England to enter the war and fight it through to the bloody end were either mercenary blackguards or blundering old fools." Wohl, p. 109.

73. _Ibid._, pp. 115-116. The words in quotation marks are the titles of Graves' social history of the period, Leonard Woolf's memoirs of the period, and Herbert Read's autobiography, which included his war diaries.

74. The title of George Dangerfield's 1935 classic on the changing British social and politics just before the Great War.

THE LORD PETER WIMSEY STORIES & WORLD WAR I

In 1935, however, the two dilemmas, peace or war, appeasement or war, had not been reached. Nearly everyone could still put his faith in the League...reinforcing [these] policies...was the pacifist movement.... It had many sources. The postwar mood of disillusionment had been revived by the war novels, plays, and autobiographies published in the late twenties.... [1]

The popularity of these [war] books spurred the republication of the war poetry that had been written during and following the World War, spurred too the production of war films (usually based on one of the...novels).... [2]

The works referred to above are, of course, what have been termed "warriors' literature." They were not the only works which used the Great War or effects of the War in some manner. These works, by those other than warriors, often reveal the opinions of the civilian population towards the war. A small subset of these works are the eleven novels and the twenty-one short stories concerning the exploits of Dorothy L. Sayers' famous sleuth, Lord Peter Wimsey. This chapter will discuss how the characters in Sayers' work dealt with the effects of the war in their lives and society. These works show the damage done to British society by the Great War, and illustrate how some of the ideas presented by the warriors' literature entered British culture even before the genre's explosion of 1928-30.

The interwar period is now regarded as being the "golden age" of the mystery story in Britain,[3] and any view of life in Britain during this time would be incomplete without the consideration of those mysteries. Or, as A. J. P. Taylor put it:

> The new development was the detective story; a sober, solid narrative in which ordinary people had extraordinary experiences–usually murder.... Certainly these stories often provide the historian clearer and more accurate social detail than can be found in more literary works.... [T]he picture of the interwar Englishman, particularly of the middle class, is incomplete, unless we see him reading... detective stories.... [4]

All of Sayers' detective fiction[5] falls very well into this definition; whether a literary party, a country vicarage, an advertising agency, a county manor, or an Oxford college, the settings all show fairly ordinary people and their reactions to "extraordinary experiences," especially the extraordinary Lord Peter. Many of the characters ring true to life, rather than being mere marionettes in the hands of the author,[6] a common problem in mysteries of the time.

The war theme is most evident in the fourth Wimsey novel, The Unpleasantness at the Bellona Club [1928]. The novel's opening scene takes place on Armistice Day evening, in the Bellona Club, Piccadilly, between Lord Peter Wimsey and an friend from the War, George Fentiman.

He [Fentiman] knew that young Marchbanks had been killed at Hill 60, and that [Colonel Marchbanks] was wont to give a small, informal dinner on Armistice night to his son's intimate friends....

"And how are things going with you?" he [Wimsey] asked.

"Oh, rotten as usual. Tummy all wrong and no money. What's the damn good of it, Wimsey? A man goes and fights for his country, gets his insides all gassed out, and loses his job, and all they give him is the privilege of marching past the Cenotaph once a year and paying four shillings in the pound." [7]

Captain George Fentiman is the first of the war-torn characters met in the Bellona Club. George's problems are shown to the reader when he lapses into hysterics when it is discovered that his grandfather, General Fentiman [a veteran of the Crimea] was not merely sleeping in front of the Bellona Club fireplace as usual, but had been dead for some time.[8] This leads into a description of what was described above as the 'us versus them habit."

It is doubtful which occurrence was more disagreeable to the senior members of the Bellona Club—the grotesque death of General Fentiman in their midst or the indecent neurasthenia of his grandson. Only the younger men felt no sense of outrage; they knew too much. Dick Challoner—known to his friends as Tin-Tummy Challoner, owing to the fact that he had been fitted with a spare part after the second battle of the Somme—took the gasping Fentiman away.... [9]

62

[And, when it was time to move the body, Captain Culyer, the Club secretary, was unable to help because he "had only one sound arm."][10]

The fact that George Fentiman was accustomed to having "attacks" quite often is soon made apparent, along with the fact that he was not the only member of the Bellona Club who was a victim of shell-shock.[11] Later in the novel, when George is being followed, his brother, Major Robert Fentiman, and Wimsey both put the idea down to part of George's "persecution-mania."[12] George's delusions come to a head in the third-to-last chapter, when his "shell-shock" blossoms into full-fledged schizophrenia.[13]

Robert was also affected by his wartime experiences, although not nearly to the extent his younger brother was. Robert was described by Wimsey early on as "Frightfully hearty and all that–regular army type."[14] Another description given later is much fuller.

"I believe Robert would cheerfully go through another five years of war and think it all a very good rag. Robert was proverbial, you know, for never turning a hair. I remember Robert, at that ghastly hole at Carency, where the whole ground was rotten with corpses–ugh!–potting those great swollen rats for a penny a time, and laughing at them. Rats. Alive and putrid with what they'd been feeding on. Oh, yes, Robert was thought a very good soldier." [15]

Robert may have been an ideal soldier, but is it likely that the qualities which made him one were well suited for peace?

The War fills The Unpleasantness at the Bellona Club. Many of the most necessary plot devices occur because of the effects of the War: the annual dinner for a lost son's friends; an annual phone call to the brother of a friend who was killed half an hour before the Armistice;[16] the extra confusion in the Bellona Club on Armistice Day because of the large number of out of town members in London for the day;[17] the absence of the regular Club doorman who was at the service at the Cenotaph;[18] etc. Even the customs of wearing a Flanders' poppy and the two-minute silence are made integral parts of the story.[19] The Unpleasantness at the Bellona Club is as much a story of the effects of the Great War on British society as it is a detective story, and shows the attitudes of the late twenties better, perhaps, than the works mentioned in the last chapter.

Yet what about the main character, Lord Peter Wimsey himself? In The Unpleasantness at the Bellona Club, Wimsey is presented as one of the mass of "us"–a veteran who understands the pressures put on a soldier like George Fentiman. Any special effects on Wimsey caused by the War are not clearly seen in this novel, but are easily seen in some of the other stories, even if the effects of the War itself were more in evidence in the Bellona Club than in other works.

Although Wimsey's character deepens throughout the series of stories, he starts out in the first novel, Whose Body? [1923], with a complete personality, one which stays consistent for the next seventeen years and which "never does an unWimseylike thing or utters an unWimseylike speech."[20] It is in Whose Body? that the effects of the war on Wimsey are first shown, for, like George Fentiman, he is a sufferer of shell-shock.

Wimsey's nervous condition was not strictly needed in the story line of Whose Body?, but it soon became a very necessary aspect of his personality. It was one of the few flaws in Wimsey's makeup, something which served to make him more believable as a person. As Wimsey's mother described it to his new wife in the last novel, Busman's Honeymoon [1937]:

> "He doesn't like responsibility, you know...and the War and one thing and another was bad for people that way.... There were eighteen months... not that he'll ever tell you about that...if he does, then you'll know he's cured.... I don't mean he went out of his head or anything...only he was so dreadfully afraid to go to sleep...and he couldn't give an order, not even to the servants.... I suppose if you've been giving orders for nearly four years to people to go and get blown to pieces it gives you...an inhibition...." [21]

Or, as a prominent "nerve specialist" who figures highly in Whose Body? put it:

> "You know quite well that the strain you put on your nerves during the war has left its mark on you. It has left what I may call old wounds in your brain...if you stimulate those damaged places... again, you run the risk of opening up the old wounds." [22]

The "nerves" from which Wimsey was to suffer for much of his career came from a variety of sources, most of which were connected with events which occurred during the War. Besides the responsibility for the life and well being of those under his command [alluded to above] the War help cause the end of Wimsey's engagement,[23] an event which he spoke about in a few of the novels with some showing pain.[24] After the engagement was broken, however, more probable causes of Wimsey's problem appear. Wimsey

> went back to his job the army with...the fixed intention of getting killed, but all he got was his majority and his D.S.O. for some recklessly good work behind the German Front. In 1918 he was... buried in shell-hole near Caudry, and that left him with a bad nervous breakdown.... [25]

It was the experiences behind the German lines[26] which he would later claim led him to choose detective work as a therapy to bring him out of the shell-shock and depression caused by his breakdown and broken engagement.[27]

There are two instances where Wimsey's war-caused nightmares are shown: the first novel and the last. In Whose Body?, the nightmares are stimulated by Wimsey's sudden realization that a respectable Harley Street doctor is behind two mysterious sets of circumstances. As Wimsey sat up late at night, mulling over the case he had just unraveled, he fell into a reverie while looking at the fire and listening to the sounds of the heavy trucks going past his flat. The next moment Wimsey was waking up his "man" [Bunter, who had been his sergeant during the war], insisting that they were back in the trenches, with enemy sappers digging at their trench.[28]

It is this scene which leads to the interview with the famous "nerve specialist" quoted above. In the novel, Wimsey recovers fairly quickly–it is made clear in this novel as well as some of the later ones that the bouts with nightmares and other reactions are only relapses–and he goes on to prove his case. After the case is closed, Wimsey appears happy with a job well done–he even plans a dinner for those who had been suspected by himself and/or the police,[29] a fairly unusual ending for a Wimsey story.

The fact that Wimsey did have some sort of reaction after the euphoria of solving his first major case is not stated outright in the opening sequences of the next novel, Clouds of Witness [1927], but that interpretation is possible. All that is said is that Wimsey had taken a three-month-long vacation to recover from "his exertion in unravelling the Battersea Mystery,"[30] but the main "exertions" he had to recover from were his nightmares.

There is little probing of Wimsey's character in Witness; the development which exists is deployed more in searching into the characters of Wimsey's friends and family. Even so, there was a minor reactions on Wimsey's part at the end. Once he had proved his brother innocent of murder, he and two of his friends went out on the town and nearly made "public spectacles" of themselves in Parliament Square.[31]

The third Wimsey novel, Unnatural Death [1927], shows what may be considered the classic Wimsey reaction to the ending of a case. It was the type of ending which could easily be read into both the be-

ginning of Clouds of Witness [dealing with the end of Whose Body?] and
its end in Parliament Square. The ending of Unnatural Death is also
consistent with Wimsey's character as shown in the nightmare sequence
and its consequences in Whose Body?[32]

From the start of the series, Wimsey is shown as being boxed in by
his early training; by what Wimsey's friend Inspector Parker called the
"playing-fields-of-Eton-complex."[33] Wimsey regarded detection as a
game, while at the same time being worried that he was not playing the
game correctly. According to Parker, Wimsey was always

> "thinking about your attitude. You want to be con-
> sistent, you want to look pretty, you want to swag-
> ger debonairly through a comedy of puppets. But
> that's childish.... You want to look dignified and
> consistent—what's that got to do with it?... Life's
> not a football match.... You can't be a
> sportsman."[34]

In Unnatural Death, this theme returns to combine with Wimsey's
nervous aversion to responsibility. Through his natural curiosity,
Wimsey reopens a mysterious death, trying to prove it was murder. His
investigations cause two further murders and three attempted murders,
as well as the suicide of the killer. Although Wimsey was relieved of
some of his guilty feelings through a conversation with a vicar, most of
those feelings remained,[35] and blend in with the end of the most violent
of Sayers' works.[36]

At first glance, it might be argued that Wimsey's actions and feeling
have little to do with his wartime experiences, but only one of the five

novels written after the Bellona Club fails to show some form of re-action,[37] even it those reactions are not blamed on the wartime exper-iences. If the entire Wimsey series as a whole is considered, however, only those wartime experiences could explain Wimsey's emotional pro-blems, and that was how Sayers herself explained them in the last two novels, Gaudy Night [1936] and Busman's Honeymoon, as well as the "Biographical Note" [1936]. These three works taken together explain Wimsey's reactions at the end of so many of his cases.

It is the "Biographical Note," "written" by Wimsey's maternal Uncle Paul, that the details of Wimsey's engagement, "burial," and subsequent breakdown and recovery are given,[38] as well as the assertion that

> Peter's intellect pulled him on way and his nerves another, till I began to be afraid they would pull him to pieces. At the end of every case we had the old nightmares and shell-shock over again.[39]

In Gaudy Night the "old nightmares and shell-shock" which Wimsey suffered at the end of his cases were allowed to come through, and the "psychology" which Sayers had provided Wimsey was allowed to surface to a certain extent. These facts are even projected backwards into some of the earlier cases.[40] Wimsey was allowed to show some of these weaknesses to the woman he had saved from the gallows in Strong Poison [1930] and had chased throughout Have His Carcase [1932]. The extent of this revelation is slight, however; just enough is shown to justify Harriet Vane's acceptance of Wimsey's last proposal. The final stripping of Wimsey's defenses and explanations of his weaknesses are left to Busman's Honeymoon.

Wimsey desires Harriet because, among other reasons, "she had the power to force him outside his defenses."[41] Those defenses were his early training at home and school,[42] which reinforced his reactions to his War experiences. As Wimsey rationalized:

> I must have a streak of my father in me. He was one of the old school—you either faced a fence of your own accord or were walloped over.... One learnt to pretend one wasn't a coward, and take out the change in bad dreams. [43]

In Busman's Honeymoon, the effects of the War on Wimsey's character are shown in more detail than in any other story, not excluding Whose Body? In Whose Body?, the nightmares were brought on by Wimsey's knowledge of the murder and the responsibility to bring the killer to justice. Any reaction afterwards was caused by that murderer's being hanged due to Wimsey's intervention. In Busman's Honeymoon, the first nightmare was caused simply because there had been a murder, and it was Wimsey's responsibility to solve it even if he would rather leave it alone for personal reasons. It is the conflict of responsibilities, between the position Wimsey had assumed as a freelance detective [of sorts], always ready to help solve any case without reward as his gesture towards society, and the responsibilities he had assumed to his bride at the beginning of the novel. It was this conflict which raised

<u>Busman's Honeymoon</u> from a mere detective story towards Sayers' oft stated goal of a novel of manners.[44]

The conflict is broached soon after the murder has been discovered, in the first of three conversations between Wimsey and Harriet on the subject. As much as Wimsey would like to leave the entire mess alone, he has accepted his role as the amateur detective as the justification for his wealth and as his proper job in society.[45] When Harriet questions the need for her new husband to investigate a murder while on their honeymoon, Wimsey can only reply:

> "I can't wash my hands of a thing, merely because it's inconvenient to my lordship.... I hate violence! I loathe wars and slaughter, and men quarrelling and fighting like beasts! Don't say it isn't my business. It's everybody's business." [46]

To break from his role would break the code of the upperclass Englishman, and that was something which Wimsey could never do.

Harriet knew perfectly well what Wimsey's self-assumed responsibilities were, as a speech she gave in <u>Gaudy Night</u> shows.[47] What she was not yet aware of in <u>Gaudy Night</u> is Wimsey's conflict over responsibility, Wimsey's hatred of violence of any sort—war, murder, hanging—which is portrayed in the last two novels. Wimsey is shown also as a man trying to avoid serious thinking about the responsibility coping with violence could bring; hence his habit of always reading, talking, working, playing cricket, driving as fast as possible, etc.–anything to occupy his mind.

> I can enjoy practically everything that comes along
> —while it's happening. Only I have to keep on
> doing things, because if I once stop, it all seems
> a lot of rot and I don't care if I go west tomorrow.
>
> But if she [Harriet] wanted an answer to her ques-
> tions about Peter, there it was, quite appallingly
> plain. He did not want to forget or to be quiet, or
> to be spared things, or to stay put. All he wanted
> was some kind of central stability, and he was ap-
> parently ready to take anything that came along,
> so long as it stimulated him to keep that
> precarious balance. [48]

The night before Wimsey solves the murder in <u>Busman's Honey-</u><u>moon</u>, the nightmares return. When questioned by Harriet the next morning, Wimsey could only try to explain, but really could not, leaving him to finish by saying: "Oh, it was only the old responsibility dream, and a mild one at that."[49]

After the murder had finally been solved, but before the trial, Harriet and the reader finally learn more about Wimsey's breakdown and recovery from his mother. First, though, Wimsey, having done his duty by catching the murderer, salves his conscience by hiring the best defense barrister in Britain. For the only time, Wimsey is shown from arrest to hanging, and his actions are consistent with those of a person bound to do his duty, and disliking every minute.[50] When the course of legal action was finished, Wimsey once again felt the responsibility of having a man sent to his death. The responsibility was similar for Wimsey—whether it was ordering men to their deaths during the War or catching murderers to be hanged. All represented people sacrificed to social principles which Wimsey felt bound to enforce.[51]

Peter Wimsey is thus portrayed by Sayers as a man filled with guilt and repressed horror stemming from his War experiences, repeating in peacetime the same general type of behavior for his society: finding, fighting, and finally killing [usually through surrogates] his society's enemies, while trying to justify his actions to himself and seeking the ever elusive "central stability."

None of the novels escape some possible tragedy caused by the War. In all of the novels of the 1920s some personal tragedy caused by or attributed to the War strikes at least one of the minor characters: in Whose Body? there is the young shell-shocked man in the doctor's office; in Clouds of Witness Ellen's Bert had been killed in the war; in the short story "The Undignified Melodrama of the Bone of Contention," Wimsey's friend Lumsden had lost a leg; it was the death in the war of John Dawson which set up the succession of events which provided the motive in Unnatural Death; and, of course, the Bellona Club novel is full of such references. The same could be said of the novels and many of the short stories from the 1930s as well.[52] In short, many of the characters of the Wimsey stories had been touched by the war, and that touch was nearly always a negative one. Yet many of these references, outside of Wimsey's own problems and many of those belonging to characters in the Bellona Club, are very casual and easily missed, which may be the best argument for their quality of reflection of the society in which they were set.

The Sayers stories do, after all, show the society of inter-war Britain very well, as comparisons with both scholarly and popular accounts of the interwar period would show. Most of that society's problems were blamed on the Great War, and contributed to the overall sense of disillusionment of the period. Many of these problems are dealt with in the following chapter, but some of the ones Sayers showed in her works are better analyzed here, at least briefly.

In Clouds of Witness, for example, the phenomenon of the radical socialist conscientious objector appears in the person of George Goyles, the use of church bells as alarms figures in The Nine Taylors [1934], and the possibilities of food rationing in the next war is mentioned in Busman's Honeymoon. Many of the social changes are given much more scope than these short references to wars past and future. One of the most important ones [and most referred to], which many people of the twenties often linked somewhat erroneously with the Great War, was the "problem of women."

Parts of this "problem" are dealt with at length in some of the novels: women in the workplace in Murder Must Advertise [1933]; women professionals in Have His Carcase [1930] and Gaudy Night; and women's education in The Nine Taylors and Gaudy Night. These areas, while part of the overall question, were not just blamed on the Great War and the changes it caused. However the question of what was called in the 1920s "the problems of the 'surplus women'"[53] was blamed on the Great War.

During the War, many women took up the jobs which the millions of men who had volunteered or had been conscripted left. When the

War was over, most of the women were turned out of their jobs, either to make room for returning men or because of the postwar recession. The problem was, as Robert Graves put it:

> Most demobilized young women therefore turned to the obvious profession of marriage; but women had slightly outnumbered men even before the war killed off one eligible man in seven and seriously injured another.... [54]

Sayers, speaking as Wimsey, put the matter differently, when Wimsey tells his friend Parker why he was using an "old maid" as an enquiry agent.

> Miss Climpson...is a manifestation of the wasteful way in which this country is run.... Thousands of old maids, simply bursting with useful energy, forced by our stupid social system into hydros and hotels and posts as companions, where their magnificent...powers...are allowed to dissipate themselves or even become harmful to the community, while the ratepayers' money is spent on getting work for which these women are providentially fitted...inefficiently carried out.... [55]

To further his own work, as well as to find useful employment for these "surplus women," Wimsey sets up a "typing bureau," which uses these women, when not on assignment from Wimsey, to investigate various crimes which exploited unsuspecting women[56] and the working classes. Wimsey called this agency "my own...insurance against the

Socialist Revolution...when it comes."[57] And there are other examples of other problems in addition to this one brief mention.

In all, a careful reading of the Wimsey stories shows that they are full of details of interwar British society, and that interwar British society was full of references and reminders of the Great War on all levels. That the War involved all segments of society can be seen just from the variety of characters who were said to have fought in the Great War–from the aristocratic Lord Peter and his brother, the Duke of Denver, to the gentrified Fentiman brothers, the gentleman cardsharper Denis Cathcart, the professional Dr. Penberthy in The Unpleasantness at the Bellona Club, the commercial Mr. Duckworthy in "The Image in the Mirror," the Scots painter Campbell in Five Red Herrings [1931], the working class in Padgett in Gaudy Night, and finally to the archetypical upstairs servant, Bunter, and a large number of others. All are shown to have had a common experience, which could at times supercede their class differences.

Yet the question remains–why? That is, why did the War occupy such a prominent place in Sayers' work; why did she treat the effects and aftermath of the War on her society in this way? There are two possible reasons: either Sayers had personal reasons to be so affected by the War that it occupied her mind almost as much as it did the warriors quoted in the second chapter; or Sayers believed the way she portrayed her society, preoccupation with the War and all, as a reasonable one, one which would be accepted by the reading public as realistic.

After all, although books attacking the War or giving negative views of it were fairly common throughout the interwar period, they did not represent the totality of opinion.[58]   A person of Sayers' background would not automatically support the negative views which the works of the front line soldiers contained.

Sayers came from what George Orwell defined as the "lower-upper-middle class"–that is, those people who could almost be defined as gentry, but who could either just barely afford to keep up appearances, or who just missed but who came from a "good" family.[59] To be specific, Sayers' father was a Church of England parson, first at Oxford and then in the country. Like many of her class and sex, Sayers was educated at home rather than at a local school until she was sixteen, when she went to a boarding school to prepare her for college [Somerville College at Oxford]. Like most children of her class, she was encouraged to play only with children of that class.[60]

From the way Sayers wrote about the War, it might be expected that she had some personal experiences during the War, such as Vera Brittain had, which might have put her in sympathy with those returning soldiers of her class, such as Carrington, Aldington, and Graves, who would write negatively about the War. Some of the scenes which Sayers created, especially in the Bellona Club, could only be written by a person who either had known tragedy because of the War or who had been deeply affected by the same climate of opinion in which the warriors were immersed.

Sayers was a student Oxford [1912-15] during the first part of the War years, and saw the changes which took place there during those first few months. She saw the men's college empty out as the students and junior faculty volunteered for the armed services, read the names of many of her Oxford contemporaries in the obituary lists; in short, Sayers had every opportunity for knowing what the effects of the War on her society were as any other intelligent civilian did.[61] That does not mean, however, that Sayers had any personal experience of the horrors which those near and at the front had to face, so this could not account for the way Sayers would portray the war in her writings.

It must be remembered that one of the most prevalent themes of the War literature genre is what has been called the "us versus them conflict." As mentioned in Chapter II, this conflict was not between "our side versus their side" but between those of the front lines and everybody else. As explained before, both the soldiers and the Government tried to keep those at home ignorant of the conditions at the front: the Government to keep morale at home as high as possible and the soldiers for the dual reasons of not causing worry for their loved ones and because they felt that those loved ones could not understand what they were going through.[62] During the War, the conditions at the Front were not really kept secret, but they were ignored and glossed over, and they could really touch only those who fought there. "They" could only learn the truth at secondhand, from those home on leave or from some of the poetry. Sayers carefully ignored the former [as will be seen below] and evidence of the later [either way] is not available.

The loss of a lover might have accounted for a great deal of interest in the conditions of the War and the War's effects on society, but that is not the case with Sayers, despite some suggestions to that effect. In fact, "the moment friendship turned to anything approaching love, Dorothy became uneasy."[63] Before the war started, there seem to have been only two men Sayers was at all interested in in any way.

> In her first few terms at Somerville, Dorothy had
> a friendship of mild intensity...[a] young man she
> met in queue.... They both wrote poems, which
> they showed each other; and discussed life in a
> serious and responsible manner. But the lasting
> friendships she made at that time were with a
> group of other first-year Somerville students.... [64]

The other man who interested Sayers at this time was Hugh Percy Allen, the director of the Bach Choir [she was a member]. Allen was not involved in the War.

Despite the War, life in Somerville remained much the same until the spring of 1915–Sayers' last semester–when Somerville was converted into a military hospital and the students moved into the [by then] half-empty Oriel College.[65] There is no evidence that this move was in any way traumatic for Sayers.

The only direct contact which Sayers had with the Great War in France occurred at the start of the War, when she was in France on holiday during the summer of 1914. It appears that she was caught up in the excitement [the possibilities of being trapped in France, etc.] rather than being in any panic,[66] and again it is fairly improbable that her "adventurette" in France would influence her writing for the next quarter century.

In general, Sayers' biographer Ralph Hone did not overstate the effects of the war on Sayers:

Dorothy's experience indicates that the lot of the young single woman in England during World War I could be relatively immune from distress. Her first volume of verse, which appeared in the very midst of the War in 1916...contains a singularly undiscerning dedication...and the poems themselves reveal no awareness beyond her fairly sheltered life in Oxford. The second volume of her verse, published in 1918, also shows an individual isolated from the larger world. [67]

This judgement is somewhat–but only somewhat–harsh. When Somerville had been converted into a hospital, Sayers had considered going to France to help her country along the lines other young women of her class, such as Vera Brittain, did, although she soon abandoned the idea.[68] Instead, after leaving Oxford, she faced the necessity of getting a job. Sayers had first returned home, but found that home dull and crowded. It was during this visit that Sayers had one of her few opportunities to see the effects of the fighting on the men who were experiencing it.

Visitors included an uncle and a cousin, both recently returned from the front: "Both have nervous breakdowns–one has neuritis, the other has damaged eyes gazing at aeroplanes. Jolly business, war! Both seem uncommonly gloomy over the prospects, but I don't know how far they can possible judge." [69]

Sayers soon left home for her first real job, a teaching job at Hull in 1916, where she was able to put together her first volume of verse.

Despite the injuries to two members of her extended family, Sayers' attitude towards the War, at least in its early stages, may be summed up by her comment made above her relatives' "gloom." In her optimism, Sayers was not unlike most of the rest of the civilian population. It was only after the winter of 1916-1917[70] that public opinion even started to echo the despair of the soldiers at the Front, and the public's despair never came close to being as deep or as widespread. So, there is no known reason why Sayers should have been deeply affected by the War while it was going on, and there is very little evidence that she was in any way affected.

In 1917 Sayers moved back to Oxford, taking a job with a small publisher. This led Sayers into meeting one of the few men who might figure into the ways Sayers portrayed Peter Wimsey and the War the way she did: Eric Whelpton.

Whelpton appeared at a crossroads in Sayers' life; she had received [and rejected] her first marriage proposal a short time before the meeting from a friend of her employer, and was also recovering from an appendicitis operation. During her recovery, she had resolved to find out if the feelings raised by her unwelcome suitor were raised by the suitor or by marriage, or, as she put it, "Have I physical horror of marriage, or just an aesthetic horror of him?"[71]

Sayers started her investigation by flirting with her doctor, but there were few other men in Oxford for with which to conduct such research until after the Armistice.[72] With the return of men to Oxford, Sayers met men like the Sitwell brothers and Sassoon at literary parties. Iron-ically, considering the use Sayers would later make of the War theme in her writing, these meetings did not come off well.[73] Whelpton was one of the returning soldiers who came to Oxford, and the one soldier who did interest Sayers.

Whelpton, who lived in the flat on the floor below Sayers at Oxford, had been invalided out of the army. There has been some debate over Whelpton's condition at this time. Janet Hitchman, in her biography of Sayers, Such a Strange Lady, claims that "The War had left him a prey to nerves and nightmares but not wounded."[74] She goes on to say that once Sayers had been introduced to Whelpton

> Miss Sayers was lost. He could not walk down the street without being panthertracked by his adorer, who could watch his comings and goings from her sitting room window.... Dorothy threw himself at him and got very little in exchange, even on the intellectual level. [75]

Hitchman does not draw the line at saying that Whelpton was, at least in part, the basis of Wimsey,[76] although she puts it a little stronger than Dawson Gaillard did in his study, Dorothy L. Sayers.

> Undoubtedly Sayers' portraits of George Fentiman and Peter Wimsey own much to Eric Whelpton.... She promised to make him famous...she did fulfill her promise, for some have speculated that Eric Whelpton is the model for Peter Wimsey. [77]

Hitchman believed that Wimsey could have been based on an Oxford lover who had been killed during the War when the introduction she wrote to Striding Folly was published in 1973.[78] By the time she published the biography of Sayers in 1975, Hitchman had not been able to discover anyone who could fit the prerequisites she had established for that wartime lover. She had, however, discovered a post-war person, whom Sayers had met at Oxford, who could be squeezed into the vacant scenario. Hence her comments above.

The argument Hitchman puts forward in favor of Whelpton's being the basis of Wimsey can best be put as follows:

> Wimsey was based for the most part on a shell-shocked lover of Sayers;
> Whelpton was shell-shocked;
> Sayers loved Whelpton;
> Whelpton was the only shell-shocked lover Sayers had before writing the first Wimsey book;
> Therefore, Whelpton was the basis for Wimsey.

Hitchman therefore asserts that Whelpton was shell-shocked and has Sayers "panthertracking" him through the streets of Oxford. Gaillard, however, states that Whelpton had been "wounded and discharged from military service,"[79] which conflicts with Hitchman's opinion of Whelpton's mental and physical condition. Both Ralph Hone and James Brabazon in their biographies [both entitled Dorothy L. Sayers] say that Whelpton was invalided out of service because of polio, which seems the most probable cause, based on the internal evidence in the biographies.[80] Hitchman is the only one who believes that Whelpton was shell-shocked, and the only reason for this seems to be that if Wimsey was based on Whelpton, he would have to be.

Three of the biographers [Hitchman, Hone, and Gaillard] assert that Sayers was in love with Whelpton, although only Hitchman describes Sayers as panthertracking Whelpton. It should be noted that Hitchman probably took the description mentioned above from Doreen Wallace, who was also attracted to Whelpton.[81] Brabazon, who as Sayers' official biographer is the only person to have access to all of Sayers' papers, believes that while Sayers was sympathetic and material in her feelings towards Whelpton–and somewhat in love with him–she did not find in Whelpton "a man who truly matched her in spirit."[82] In other words, it is unlikely that Whelpton would inspire Sayers to fashion Wimsey totally in his likeness.

In fact, it is probable that Wimsey was a combination of Sayers herself and her dream lover.[83] If that is the case, then the treatment Sayers gave the Great War in the Wimsey stories did not depend on any personal experiences which Sayers had or shared. Sayers did not visit the Front or do any nursing. Sayers did not have a lover or favorite relative killed or maimed. In short, there are no reasons for believing that the War left any of the types of psychological scars on Sayers which might account for the way Sayers' treatment of the War and its veterans matched those of the warriors.

There remain some other possible reasons for the way Sayers treated the aftermath of the Great War which should be disposed with before going on. One possible reason could have been Sayers' religious conviction. She was the only child of an Anglican minister, held deep religious convictions, and once was almost as well-known for her religious plays and translation of Dante as she was for her mysteries.

There are no real indications, however, that Sayers was ever a religious pacifist, or any other type of pacifist. During World War II, Sayers volunteered to work on the Authors' Planning Committee of the Ministry of Information. According to Brabazon:

> On the whole Dorothy met the war with exultation. Within the bulky frame of this upper middle-class English-woman there still lived the Musketeer soul. Dorothy's patriotism, her sense of history and her sense of romance...responded to the image...of the little peaceable island standing as a bulwark against tyranny.... [84]

Sayers also produced a short work commenting on the war [Begin Here] at the socialist publisher Victor Gollancz' request. Brabazon believes that this work shows that

> [a]nother type of Christian might have mourned the folly of man, the loss of life, the break-up of homes...and the disruption that the war would surely bring. Not Dorothy. Providence had given her a powerful case to argue, and nothing could suit her better. The work of Christ and His Church was...to bring good out of evil....what harm was there in a little shortlived suffering...if it gave her the chance to prove it? [85]

The above is hardly the description of a Christian pacifist.

Had Sayers' career started with the publication of <u>Unnatural Death</u> in late 1927, followed by <u>The Unpleasantness at the Bellona Club</u> as the second novel, the genesis of Sayers' use of the war and Wimsey's war experiences would be easily explained. First of all, Hitchman would easily have found her shell-shocked lover for Sayers, as Sayers had met and married Captain Oswald Atherton "Mac" Fleming during the spring of 1926.[86] Mac was not seriously shell-shocked, but as time went on, he was less and less able to work steadily.[87]

Second, and perhaps more importantly, was the time-frame. 1928 was the first year of the three-year deluge of the warrior' literature. Four of the main works which appeared in 1928 were: Blunden's <u>Undertones of War</u>; Sassoon's <u>Memoirs of a Fox Hunting Man</u>; Remarque's <u>All Quiet on the Western Front</u>; and the first performance of Sheriff's <u>Journey's End</u>. A glance through the "Times Literary Supplement" which reviewed <u>The Unpleasantness at the Bellona Club</u> [August 16, 1928] shows reviews of two war memoirs [<u>Was it Yesterday</u> by A. M. Brown and <u>Medicine and Duty: a War Diary</u> by Harold Deardon], two reviews of war histories [<u>British Documents on the Origins of the War 1898-1914</u> edited by G. P. Gooch and Harold Temperly, and <u>Economic and Social History of the World War</u> published by the Oxford University Press], as well as an advertisement for Sir George Arthur's biography of Lord Haig.

In such a context, <u>The Unpleasantness at the Bellona Club</u> makes perfect sense. As Fussell said apropos of another matter, "Everyone writes for an audience,"[88] and to judge the type of books selling in 1928, and the great success of the warriors' literature in general, the War themes of the <u>Bellona Club</u> fit right in with what the audience wanted.

In such a context [Unnatural Death and Bellona Club being the first two Wimsey novels] Wimsey would have been easily explained away as being somewhat based on Sayers' husband, and Wimsey's conflicts and the terrible injuries [mental and physical] of the Bellona Club members would have been shown to have mostly stemmed from Mac and his war stories and friends, and the wave of War books which were starting to appear.

This, of course, was not the case. By the time Unnatural Death was published, there were already two Wimsey novels and a number of short stories. Wimsey was already shown to be suffering from shell-shock, Denis Cathcart had already been ruined by the war,[89] and all the other minor tragedies and incidents connected with the war were on record. Wimsey was already the character who "never does an unWimseylike thing or utters an unWimseylike speech."[90] By the time the surge of war memoirs started in 1928, the way Sayers would show the War was already set.

Some of the works from the period 1928-30 caused outrage [as was noted in the previous chapter]. Perhaps it is best to add another quote from the warrior and literary critic A. C. Ward about this controversy:

> Such facts hurt the public conscience so badly that attempts are made to salve the hurt by declaring that the facts are not as stated; or that the publication of those facts is a libel on the British army, whereas it is, actually, no more than the record of what happened to certain individual men....[91]

Since the works from the period 1928-30 raised the most controversy, and contain some of the best works of the genre, it is natural that much of the attention the genre gets is focused on these works, and occupies such a large place in the intellectual historiography of interwar Britain. These works should not be viewed as coming out of a complete vacuum, however. Some of what are now recognized as major works [especially the poetry] came out during the War, and some between the years 1918 and 1928. In addition to these semi-underground works, the years 1918 to 1928 were also the time when the warriors were mulling over the War and trying to adjust their experiences in it to the post-war world. It is from these early works and any talk she may have overheard that Sayers formed the attitudes from her characters. The quick success of the works of 1928-30 shows that the public as prepared for them, and it should not be surprising that a fringe member of Bloomsbury like Sayers would have captured the tone of her times.

This does not mean that Sayers herself had any of these attitudes. Sayers followed Dr. Johnson's dictum "No man but a blockhead ever wrote, except for money" when it came to her detective stories.[92] Since it was said that "every Englishman loves a lord," her detective became one. Since the custom of most English detective fiction called for an amateur detective, Wimsey became the impartial amateur who helped his society and country. Since it was easier, and more fun, to write about amateur detectives who were well off,[93] Wimsey was made the only brother of the Duke of Denver, the wealthiest peer in Britain and personally worth over £500,000.[94] And since Wimsey was the proper age [b. 1890], he was given a magnificent and fairly probable war record, complete with the possible effects service in the War might have caused to his character.

There is no need to invent shell-shocked lovers, or any of the other causes suggested for why Sayers wrote Wimsey the way she did. There is no need to go further than the society Sayers was writing out of, the audience she was writing for, her experience in an ad agency [she is, after all, the person often given credit for the slogan "it pays to advertise"], and the success of her work to see that Sayers wrote detective stories that sold, and sold at least in part because she knew what the public would buy, and believe. The Great War and its horrors were part of the British psyche even before the works of 1928-1930 brought it to the surface.

NOTES

1. Mowat, p. 537.

2. Joyce Berkman, "Pacificism in England: 1914-1939" [Yale Dissertation, 1967], pp. 102-103. For more details, see pp. 102-125.

3. The 1920s in Britain were quickly recognized as "the golden age," as a chapter title in Howard Haycroft's Murder for Pleasure [New York, 1943] shows. The time period has been extended by some authors to the 1930s as well; Dawson Gaillard, Dorothy L. Sayers [New York, 1981], p. 3.

4. Taylor, 1914-1945, p. 312. One example of "the Englishman and his mystery," although from the middle class, was Sir Nevile Henderson, Chamberlain's ambassador to Berlin. While describing his activities at the 1938 Nuremberg rally [in the midst of the Czech crisis], Henderson mentions that he was forced to send a message on "the blank pages torn from some detective stories which I happened to have taken with me." Unfortunately the titles are not known. Sir Nevile Henderson, Failure of a Mission [New York, 1940], pp. 148-149.

5. The one non-Wimsey novel, The Documents in the Case, twenty-two other short detective stories, and all of Sayers' later work will not be considered. All further references to Sayers' work in general terms shall only apply to Wimsey stories.

6. This despite Edmund Wilson's well known comments on Sayers' "conventional English village characters" and "dreadful stock English nobleman." Edmund Wilson, A Literary Chronicle: 1920-1950 [New York, 1956], p. 341. Wilson has three articles on detective fiction in this anthology, all attacking the entire genre except for a few kind references to A. Conan Doyle. It may be assumed that Sayers, a product of an English country vicarage, might know more about English village life than the literary snob and critic for the New Yorker. "But in a village—no matter what

village–they were all immutable...parson, organist, sweep, duke's son, doctor's daughter, moving like chessman upon their alloted squares." Dorothy L. Sayers, <u>Busman's Honeymoon</u> [New York, 1968], p. 82.

7. Dorothy L. Sayers, <u>The Unpleasantness at the Bellona Club</u> [New York, 1963], pp. 7-8.

8. <u>Ibid</u>., p. 10.

9. <u>Bellona Club</u>, p. 10.

10. <u>Ibid</u>., p. 12.

11. <u>Ibid</u>., pp. 29-30.

12. <u>Ibid</u>., pp. 61-63.

13. <u>Ibid</u>., pp. 181-184.

14. <u>Ibid</u>., p. 16. Robert was still in the army, while George was using his rank as a sort of courtesy title.

15. <u>Ibid</u>., p. 75. See the Richard Aldington poem "LIVING SEPULCHERS" in <u>The Complete Poems of Richard Aldington</u> [London, 1948], p. 86.

16. <u>Bellona Club</u>, p. 17.

17. <u>Ibid</u>., pp. 34-35.

18. <u>Ibid</u>., p. 24. The cenotaph [empty tomb] is the main monument in Britain for the dead of the Great War, and the ceremony there was, and still is, attended by the members of the Royal family.

19. <u>Ibid</u>., pp. 93, 97-98.

20. Janet Hitchman, "Introduction" to Dorothy L. Sayers' <u>Striding Folly</u> [Sevenoaks, Kent, 1972], p. 14.

21. <u>Busman's Honeymoon</u>, pp. 304-305. Most of the punctuations in the speech exist because of the Duchess' mode of speech.

22. Dorothy L. Sayers, Whose Body? [New York, 1961], p. 166.

23. Some details of that engagement are found in Dorothy L. Sayers, "Biographical Note" in Unnatural Death [New York, 1955], p. ix.

24. Dorothy L. Sayers, Clouds of Witness [New York, 1966], pp. 38-39; and Bellona Club, p. 170.

25. "Note," pp. ix-x. There are other nervous habits Wimsey has, some of which are best shown in Busman's Honeymoon and The Nine Taylors [New York, 1962].

26. Mentioned in the first Wimsey story, Whose Body?, p. 163.

27. Ibid., pp. 119, 165; Strong Poison [New York, 1967], p. 97.

28. Whose Body?, pp. 130-131.

29. Ibid., pp. 191-192.

30. Clouds of Witness, p. 7.

31. Ibid., pp. 222-224.

32. Whose Body?, pp. 119-121, 125-134, 163-167.

33. Ibid., p. 120.

34. Ibid., p. 121.

35. Unnatural Death, pp. 189-191.

36. Ibid, p. 240.

37. Some examples would be in Dorothy L. Sayers, Have His Carcase [New York, 1968], pp. 350-351; Murder Must Advertise [London, 1969], pp. 251-252; and Five Red Herrings [New York, 1968], pp. 261, 276, 283. In fact, there are some sort of examples in all the Wimsey novels except Strong Poison, where Wimsey's fear of success [getting the murderer hanged] was overridden by his fear that Harriet would be found guilty instead.

38. First mentioned in Clouds of Witness, pp. 192-193.

39. "Note," p. x.

40. Such as the reference to Murder Must Advertise in Gaudy Night [New York, 1968], p. 56.

41. Ibid., p. 304.

42. For some references to Wimsey's public school code, see Whose Body?, pp. 119-121, 160-161; and Unnatural Death, pp. 189-191.

43. Busman's Honeymoon, p. 207.

44. Gaillard, pp. 27-28; also the many discussions of Sayers in Hanna Charney's The Detective Novel of Manners [London, 1981].

45. For the example of the justification of Wimsey's wealth, see Unnatural Death, pp. 36-37; for comments on Wimsey's "job," see "Note" p. xi; Clouds of Witness, pp. 142-143; Busman's Honeymoon, pp. 243-247.

46. Busman's Honeymoon, p. 107.

47. Gaudy Night, p. 33.

48. The first quote is from Busman's Honeymoon, p. 210; the second is from Gaudy Night, p. 304.

49. Busman's Honeymoon, p. 260.

50. Busman's Honeymoon, pp. 292-314. Although Wimsey always felt he had to discover the criminal, he did not always feel he had to insist upon his solution. For example, see "The Unsolved Puzzle of the Man with No Face."

51. For example Gaudy Night, pp. 282-283, and Busman's Honeymoon, p. 107.

52. Such as: Campbell and some of the others in Red Herrings; Deacon and M. Rozier in The Nine Taylors; Padgett in Gaudy Night; and many others.

53. Graves, Week-End, p. 45.

4. <u>Ibid</u>.

5. <u>Unnatural Death</u>, pp. 36-37.

6. <u>Strong Poison</u>, pp. 40-41.

7. <u>Unnatural Death</u>, p. 37.

8. See chapter II, especially those notes concerning Fussell and Bergonzi.

9. George Orwell, <u>The Road to Wigan Pier</u> [New York, 1958], pp. 60-61.

0. The best biography to date is the official biography by James Brabazon, <u>Dorothy L. Sayers</u> [New York, 1982].

1. Brabazon, p. 53.

2. Fussell, p. 79-90, especially pp. 86-90.

3. Brabazon, p. 45.

4. <u>Ibid</u>., p. 44. It should be remembered that all Somerville students were female.

5. <u>Ibid</u>., p. 53.

6. <u>Ibid</u>., pp. 51-52.

7. Ralph E. Hone, <u>Dorothy L. Sayers</u> [Kent, Ohio, 1979], p. 16.

8. Brabazon, p. 53. This contradicts Janet Hitchman's contention that Sayers never intended to go to France as a nurse. Janet Hitchman, <u>Such a Strange Lady</u> [New York, 1976], p. 29.

69. Brabazon, p. 58.

70. That is, after the terrible year of 1916 had sapped the morale of the army and the home front, and many saw the war going on forever.

71. Brabazon, p. 63.

72. <u>Ibid.</u>, pp. 63-64. Just before the Armistice, Sayers was struck down by Spanish Influenza in the epidemic which was in some ways a pandemic. Sayers only had a mild case, however.

73. <u>Ibid.</u>, p. 70.

74. Hitchman, p. 43.

75. <u>Ibid.</u>, p. 45.

76. <u>Ibid.</u>, pp. 75-76.

77. Gaillard, p. 4.

78. "Introduction," pp. 14-15.

79. Gaillard, p. 4.

80. Hone, p. 28; Brabazon, p. 70. Hone does not mention either the Whelpton–Wimsey or the Whelpton–Fentiman connections, preferring, for some reason, to equate Whelpton with the card-sharping Denis Cathcart. Hone, p. 34.

81. Hitchman does not say where she got the description of Sayers "panthertracking" Whelpton, although she does say that Sayers' relationship with Whelpton ruined her friendship with Wallace, Hitchman, pp. 44-45. Both Hone [p. 33] and Brabazon [p. 71] say Hitchman got the story from Wallace's reminiscences. Neither cite their source. In general, Hitchman, whose work was the first biography of Sayers, is generally the most unreliable, containing many errors about the stories and many misinterpretations.

82. Brabazon, pp. 71-72.

83. <u>Ibid</u>.

84. <u>Ibid.</u>, p. 176.

85. <u>Ibid.</u>, pp. 178-179.

86. <u>Ibid.</u> Sayers met Mac after August 1925 [p. 113] and married him in April 1926 [p. 117].

7. "His journalism...prospered...he was a correspondent of the 'News of the World.'"... Brabazon, p. 115.

    "At this time...Mac was not the penniless ne'er-do-well he has been painted.... In his own profession he was highly regarded...." Ibid., p. 139.

    "Mac's health began to deteriorate.... By the summer of 1928 he no longer had his job...." Ibid., pp. 139-140. Compare this to Hitchman, pp. 60-63.

8. Paul Fussell, "Writing in Wartime: the Uses of Innocence" delivered October 26, 1983, SUNY at Binghamton.

9. It should be noted that Clouds of Witness, although not published until 1927, was completed in 1925 and was meant to be a sequel to Whose Body?

0. Hitchman, p. 21.

1. Ward, p. 145.

2. Brabazon, p. 119.

3. Dorothy L. Sayers, "How I came to Invent the Character of Lord Peter" [Harcourt Brace News, July 15, 1936], pp. 1-2.

4. Lord Peter Views the Body, p. 227 ["The Adventurous Exploit in the Cave of Ali Baba"].

INTERWAR BRITISH MENTALITÉ

Generalizations in history are, of course, dangerous to make. Even though the warriors' literature had a great deal of influence on British attitudes towards war as well as British mentalité in general, this literature, and the opinions which lay behind it, was only a part of the overall Weltanschauung of interwar Britain. Although periods where one Weltanschauung prevails are rarer in history than is commonly thought, especially when crossing social and class boundaries, interwar Britain was such a period. Although it may be found in various guises, and for various reasons, there can be little doubt that the prevailing mood of the period was one of disillusionment, disenchantment, and at times, despair.

Although it is impossible to show the universality of such an outlook, let alone its causes, this chapter will show the viability and utility for assuming its existence. In addition, the interrelationship between the factors behind this Weltanschauung caused by the War and those not related to the War will be shown, as well as the cumulative effect of this outlook on the issues of war and peace.

It was popular during the interwar period, as well as afterwards, to put the blame for most of the changes in society, attitudes, and morals on the War. The preoccupation of social and intellectual historians with the "highbrow" literary evidence has helped maintain this view, even though it has not remained unchallenged, even within some of the works themselves. Far too many people were caught up in the shared disillusionment of the interwar period to have all been "scarred" by the War. It is sometimes difficult, however, to be certain to which group a person might have belonged.

> I have noticed...a certain tendency among contemporary...writers to class me with the generation that was "ineradicably scarred by the war." They have found, upon analyzing my plays, a dreadful nerve-racked cynicism, obviously the heritage of those four black years, and I have searched myself carefully to discover any grounds for believing this dramatic implication to be true. I have none. [1]

The speaker of the above paragraph may be thought of as a symbol of the problem of British disillusionment. Noel Coward was, after all, one of the symbols of that disillusionment itself. Coward may be correct when he denies that his disenchantment was not caused by the War. It is certain that he never saw action–he suffered a nervous breakdown in the army long before he was even due to be sent to France.[2] Coward was scarred by the War, but not nearly as badly as many of its true veterans.

Like Coward,[3] British society sustained a few hard knocks in the years right after the War. Unlike Coward, who became successful in the mid-twenties, the early 1920s were just the start of Britain's problems. The period since 1914 has been a time of adjustment for the British from the Great Power it was to the status of the second rank power it is. The interwar period was the start of this adjustment, even though very few people realized it at the time. It would take the next world war to shock the British, especially the English, out of their air of superiority, at least partially.

To do the English justice, they had been in reality a Great Power for just over two hundred years when the Great War broke out, and had been one in their own minds since at least the days of Edward III, if not from those of Alfred. Although the historian today realizes that this belief of at least 600 years of triumph is at best a gross exaggeration, most English have never been historians. In English popular history [some of it written by professional historians], the defeats the English have suffered since the end of the Hundred Years War have either been transformed into victories or romanticized into respectability, and sometimes both.[4] In a like manner, the recurrent economic lows were buried behind the good times. Even if it is true that the Victorian/Edwardian facade was coming apart in the years just before the War,[5] few people seem to have realized the fact. It took the War, with its huge losses, uncertainties, and discomforts, along with the literature about it which bore so little resemblance to the patriotic war literature of the past, to really begin to shake that great English complacency which had become famous during the previous century.

If the British were full of illusions about their position in the world in July 1914, some of those illusions were swept away during the War, and many others followed during the interwar years. For example, the voting public refused to believe that Britain's economic supremacy was coming to an end, and industrial supremacy had already been lost, at the turn of the century. This disbelief contributed to the Conservative Party's huge defeat in the "free trade" election of 1905. The public also refused to believe economic supremacy had been lost, mainly because of the War, to the United States in the early 1920s, and the Conservative Party again lost an election in large part due to the issue of free trade in 1923. The Conservative Party finally ended free trade at the height of the Great Depression in 1932, over thirty years after Britain's industrial supremacy had been lost to Germany and the United States. This time-lag between reality and acceptance is typical of twentieth-century Britain.

Even though the War and the many problems of the interwar years forced the British to begin to question their beliefs about what the new status quo was and their place in it, that is only half the equation. The other half was how the British replaced those illusions they were forced to give up or modify, if they were able to do so at all. In fact, although voices pointing out the many problems of interwar Britain were very common, and many other problems were so evident that they needed very little enumeration, no authoritative voice or group of voices came forward to posit solutions, even if some politicians and a few political theorists [mostly on the left] tried to fill the void. In short, while many members of the British public felt that their society was changing, few had any idea where those changes were leading, where they wanted their society to go, and how to get it to go there. The nature of interwar Britain's problems indicated that something had to be done, as the old society began breaking up, and nothing obvious came forward to replace it.

Looking backwards, the British had a number of social problems with which to be concerned. They had just gone through over four years of war in which some 700,000 Britons had died,[6] while many times that number bore physical and psychological scars from it. The British public had been under great strain during those years of war, having to endure the news—or fear of the news—that their young men had been killed, wounded, or were missing; and had also experienced rationing, spy scares, hysteria, huge defeats, etc. After the War, the public and the warriors were ready to reap the rewards which had been promised them. Lloyd George and his Liberal/Conservative coalition promised a "home fit for heroes," and the public expected a Britain and a world fit for heroes as well. The returning soldiers expected that their sacrifices and those of their friends had been worth something besides profits to a small group of war profiteers. The warriors expected to be rewarded with honor, jobs, and a better world. At best, they received some of the honor.

The promises of a rebuilt and revitalized Britain were impossible for Lloyd George and his coalition to keep. It would have taken a booming British economy with a strong Liberal or Labour government willing to exercise planning and control over it, as well as a booming world market, for those promises to be kept. The Coalition Government, which con-sisted of the Conservative Party and about half the Liberal Party, did not have the philosophical commitment to change and control which would have been needed to make Britain over. Even if some of the Liberal members hoped to bring about the type of changes necessary, the Con-servatives held 338 seats after the 1918 election, a majority not only in the Coalition, but in the House of Commons as well.[7]

The year 1919 was something of a boom year, and although the Coalition was not moving very fast, the "boomlet" gave people some hope for better times. The collapse of the postwar British economy began in April 1920, and the Government instituted deflationary measures, which, along with the loss of overseas investments during the war years, poor investments during those same years, and wild speculations during 1919, put Britain into a recession which only started to end just as the Great Depression became worldwide.[8] The Coalition, and the other interwar governments, did not have the pleasure of building many homes fit for heroes. Instead, ways had to be found to feed the unemployed former heroes while Britain struggled through economic problems which some experts think have continued until the present day.

The exact power struggles between the political parties are not relevant enough to this study to detail, but some of the general outcomes should be noted. Because of internal problems and the determination of both the Labour and Conservative parties to destroy it, the Liberal Party was eliminated as a major force after the 1929 election [if not before], although liberalism has remained a powerful force in British politics. It must be supposed that much of the electoral support the Liberals lost went to the Conservative Party during the interwar years, since the Labour Party only had four years of minority rule, while the Conservatives had six years of majority rule and eleven under the disguises of various coalitions.[9] The Conservatives polled the most votes in every interwar general election, and won the most seats in each of those elections except 1929.[10]

This reliance on the Conservatives may indicate a longing for the nonexistent but well-ordered past, rather than any support for the general policies of Stanley Baldwin and the Conservative Party.[11] Had the public desired a new or a reformed society, the Labour Party may have fared better, and even might have won the type of victory which they later won in 1945. The interpretation of the Conservative success which cannot be given is that most of the British population was satisfied with the status quo, since the Conservatives never polled a majority of the votes. In addition, there were at least three general groups which were not at all happy with their lot in interwar society, even if the cause of their discontent and disillusionment came from different causes. The restlessness of these three groups added to the notion of the disillusioned 1920s and the despairing 1930s, and they therefore deserve some mention, however slight.

The most peripheral group was what would now be called "the women's movement." The women's movement existed in Britain long before the start of World War I, when it became identified as the women's suffrage movement, and has continued in Britain until the time of this writing, suffering many ups and downs. The Great War helped speed up the acceptance of the suffrage movement's main goal, although perhaps not in a form most supporters wanted. All male citizens over the age of 21 and females over the age of 30 who met residency requirements were given the vote in 1918, which effectively tripled the vote.[12] Neither lower class male voters nor the new female voters were enfranchised on democratic principles, but as a reward for their war efforts. As Asquith, the former Prime Minister, said:

104

> Some years ago I...use[d] the expression. "Let the
> women work out their own salvation." Well, Sir,
> they have worked it out during this war. [13]

Few people could dispute this argument, even if many did not like the end result. According to figures given by A. J. P. Taylor, during the War 200,000 women took government jobs; 500,000 entered the agricultural workforce; 500,000 entered private clerical staffs; 800,000 joined the industrial workforce; and 200,000 went into the armed services or the V.A.D. At the same time, some 400,000 women left domestic service.[14] Although many women left the workforce after the War, especially in the industrial sector, others did not, and many who left were forced out either to make room for returning servicemen, to pacify the unions, or, after 1920, because of the recession. Women were still established in middle-class jobs, however, even if on the lower rungs of the middle-class ladder. As Taylor put it:

> The male clerk with his quill pen and copperplate
> handwriting had gone for good. The female short-
> hand-typist took his place. It was a decisive
> moment in women's emancipation. [15]

Even if there were complaints about this new order of things, it was there to stay, and was, in fact, only the beginning.[16]

Likewise, women now had a greater appearance in freedom. Corsets were nearly gone, and women now wore makeup, freer clothes, and short hair, went about unchaperoned, and smoked in public.[17] Some groups and many individuals fought against this "defeminization" of women, especially during the 1920s. With the high unemployment rate, women were often "represented as vampires who deprived men of their rightful jobs,"[18] although it is doubtful that many unemployed coal miners or steel workers would have taken jobs as clerks, secretaries, or helpers in tea shops, Lyons, dress shops, or the new Woolworth type stores, which, along with unskilled factory work, were the most common non-domestic jobs women held in the interwar period. Some men were, of course, displaced, but not many. This was especially true of skilled jobs.

The struggle of women towards equality was only starting in the period being considered in this study, and the progress which they have made, and have failed to make, lies outside of its ken. The problems which the start of the process caused, or which it was supposed to have caused, are worth mentioning, however. Although women as a group cannot be classified as either disillusioned or disenchanted, some women may have felt so when the progress in the women's movement, which started during the War, failed to keep its momentum afterwards, for although the types of jobs women could hold increased slightly [and the numbers in them increased greatly] the status of women in British society did not really change very much between 1919 and 1939. Others, both men and women, became disillusioned in the literal meaning of the word when this "defeminization" started. The "Women Question" [or "Problem"] is frequently seen in the interwar attempts at social history.[19] So this belief in the changing status of women's roles may be regarded as a sign of the state of flux which British society was experiencing during the interwar period, as the change in these roles did not satisfy anyone, going too far for some and not far enough for others.

The change in the status of women in British society showed in many ways. In the context of the various pacifist and antiwar groups which existed in the interwar years, for example, the importance of women in politics, especially on the local level, cannot be overstressed, even if it was undervalued at the time. Instead, as has been remarked, the main notice paid to women in the popular press and social commentaries concerned the lack of servants and women taking away men's jobs. The entrance of women into the skilled labor market during the War had caused tensions with the unions at the time, and continued to do so after the War, when employers tried to keep union labor out, although more often in favor of unskilled [or at least unrepresented] male or mixed labor than purely female labor. Even if the actual role of women in this dilution of skilled, unionized, labor was much less than claimed at the time, the important fact was that it was claimed at all.

In any event, the perceived problem of women in the work-place was not the only sign that organized labor did not find the interwar period a golden age. During the War, unions had been forced to accept the dilution of skilled labor in order to meet the demands for both man-power and material. This was, of course, agreed to only as a temporary measure, and some union and Labour Party leaders may have gotten some satisfaction out of knowing that many industries, including two of their main bete nôirs [coal mines and transportation] were also under fairly strict Government control.[20] After the War, however, the controlled industries were turned back into private hands, while many industrialists hoped to keep the advantages which had been given to them during the war years when it came to dealing with labor. Trapped quickly between a recession on the one hand and pressures from industries on the other, the unions were forced to be on the defensive throughout the interwar period.

At first, however, the unions had reasons to hope that they were entering into a golden age of unionism as the War ended. The Labour party was gaining in strength, and at first there was a postwar boom, giving rise to hopes of increased political and economic power. Therefore, just after the War, the unions were able to fight the pressures industry put on them by striking, and the period between the end of the War and 1922 saw a hugh number of strikes.[21] The unions were able to exert this counterpressure because of two reasons, the more important of which was that union membership was at an all time high, some 8,300,000 members [about 45% of the eligible membership] in 1920. The other was held in reserve: the so-called great threat of a national general strike. Unfortunately, the 1920 membership was the high for the interwar years. Membership in unions fell as the recession grew, and this in turn lessened the amount of money in the strike funds. The years between 1922 and 1926 saw union attempts to negotiate with both industry and government, especially in the area of the mining industry. Although the coal miners won some important short-term victories, the mine owners won the war, which in turn led to the use of the general strike in 1926, and complete defeat for the union/Labour side.[22]

The title which Robert Graves gave to his chapter on the General Strike in his social history of the interwar period, "Revolution Again

Averted, 1926," is very overdramatized. It shows how seriously the Strike was taken by the upper classes at the time, however. Despite the fact that the General Strike split Britain on class and political lines for a time, it was an even greater failure as a revolution, which few on the left intended it to be, than it was a strike. It did mark, however, a hardening of political attitudes. Compromise between the political right and left, if it had ever been possible, was close to impossible between 1926 and 1940. When Ramsey MacDonald tried to form a National Government of all parties in 1931, he should have realized that many of his followers, who had stronger ties to the labor movement [and apparently longer memories] than MacDonald, would refuse to follow him.

For the unions, the General Strike was supposed to be their trump card, the instrument which would keep industry in line and force the Conservative Government to pay attention to the great problems which were facing the working people of Britain. Instead, the idea of a national strike, which had been of some deterrent value, was destroyed as an effective weapon for some time, because of the incompetent management of the both the union and Labour Party leaders, and the very good planning of the Government.[23] On the other hand, the failure of the Strike drove unions and the Labour Party closer together [when it could have easily driven them apart], a fact which would prove essential when MacDonald tried to make common cause with the Conservatives in 1931.

The interwar period for the working classes was a time of despair rather than disillusionment. The main cause of labor/industrial disputes was not so much the greed of either side, but the hard times which most Britons faced in one form or another. Unemployment was high in Britain throughout the interwar period,[24] and the Great Depression was only a continuance of the postwar recession in many parts of Britain. In fact, the interwar period in Britain is also known as the "Slump." After Germany the United States, Britain was probably the hardest hit nation during the Depression.

The world of the working classes was changed at least as much as the upper classes' during the War years, and, of course, the bulk of the fighting men had been comprised of men from the working classes and lower middle class, who had faced the same dangers and many of the same pressures that their officers had. Most of the pressures, experiences, and societal changes which could have [and have] been brought forth in the social histories and commentaries to explain why the upper classes so often painted themselves as either a disillusioned and lost generation [the War generation] or as a disenchanted and apathetic generation [the postwar generation] could be just as easily be extended to apply to the working class and lower middle classes. In addition, however, the members of the lower classes did not have to worry about the genteel poverty and loss of status which members of the so-called "new poor"[25] had to face, but actual poverty and, at times, possible starvation.

This last point is important, since so much of the evidence of interwar disillusionment came from the upper classes. Most of the work concerning the working classes, especially the poorest of them, deals more with unemployment and poverty issues rather than wider issues of intellectual values. For people struggling to live, the issues were life and death of the body, not estrangement from an intellectualized ideal. The poor hoped for jobs, and food and shelter for their families, not an ideal place in a society that catered to their emotional needs. For all the space devoted to the themes of interwar disillusionment, Welstschmerz, disenchantment, etc., to the contrary [including most of this work], it should be remembered that the cause of the disillusionment and apathy of a small but significant part of British society was grinding poverty for the entire interwar period.

It was important to make the above point before going on to the next group, one which has become as much a symbol of interwar disillusionment as the warriors. Although numerically a great deal smaller than the poverty-stricken portion of the population mentioned above, this was the group which for a time in the mid-to-late 1920s held the headlines in the popular press and periodicals such as News of the World, and to which so much space in the old-style social histories was devoted. This group was identified in the popular press [and social histories] with nightclubs, cocktails, drugs, divorce, jazz, Noel Coward, Beverley Nichols, and Evelyn Waugh, and those who devoted their time to the nightclubs and wild parties were written about by the above-named authors are usually known as the "Bright Young Things" or "Bright Young People."[26]

Nothing could be more different than the lives of the ten percent or so of the British population which lived at the starvation level and the lives of the Bright Young Things, who were well off, or who were supported by those who were very well off. Unlike the warriors, who were disillusioned over what they had seen, and bemoaning their lost youth, or the poor, who were in the depths of despair caused by their existence

near starvation, the Bright Young Things went past them in their disillusionment with life, and far past the vague discontent which seems to
have gripped the general populace of Britain throughout the interwar
period as a response first to the war fever which had held them during
the First World War and then as disbelief as the Second came closer.
The Bright Young Things claimed to be bored and tired with everything,
a state of affairs which could not lead them to want to change society but
only to a quest for amusement while the boring game of life went on.

> [I]t never occurred to the Bright Young People of
> Mayfair that the most shocking thing about them
> was their completely self-centered view of life. Not
> since the post-war era of the Regency society had
> the frivolous pursuit of pleasure so blinded those
> who set the pace.... Even the opulent Edwardian
> aristocracy had...some good works among the
> working classes. Now, except for some hilarious
> charity shows...there was never any thought of
> what was happening.... Poverty and social
> injustice were ignored. [27]

The author could have added foreign affairs [or any other issue] to that
list.

　　This critique, written in the middle of what is now known as the "me
decade" of the 1970s, is more than borne out by the contemporary social
commentators. In the 1932 book Just the Other Day, in a chapter devoted to the doings of the Bright Young People,[28] the authors included
the following assessment of the group, after having presented a press
column on the infamous "baby party."

By this time it had become apparent that the standards of vulgarity were not what they had been. With the evasion of the limitations of age and sex went further freedoms. Responsibilities to class...was found as great a nuisance as any other responsibility. Politeness...is an hypocrisy, the fraudulent pretense of the civilized man that he is not ruled by greed, lust, and fear; and the only virtue claimed by the young was a negative one—they thought they were not hypocrites. [29]

Robert Graves, in his interwar social history The Long Week-end, quotes two examples of what these young members of the upper classes were supposed to act like, according to the "advanced" novelists of the 1920s and the tabloids.

"You're a modern woman. You can't love properly as the beasts do, and they're the only creatures that know. You can't live with strong men, because you're damned if you're going to be ruled; and you can't live with a weak man because you're damned if you're going to be bothered to manage them...."

"The Modern Girl's Brother."... was said to be weary, anaemic, feminine, bloodless, dolled up like a girl and an exquisite without masculinity; he resembled a silken-coated lapdog, but 'it is not suggested that he is sexually depraved.' [30]

Mowat, in his extensive work on interwar Britain, did not leave out his observations on the Bright Young People:

> Entertainment the bright young things found in
> a hectic round of parties, visits to the night
> clubs...gate-crashing other people's parties,
> speeding hither and yon in fast sporting cars....
> People were continuously 'popping' in and out of
> bed with new bed-fellows, though not...getting
> much pleasure out of it.... [31]

The actions of this group of bored, rich, spoiled, young people might have been ignored at the time, but they were not. They appear with great regularity in the contemporary social histories,[32] and they populate the plays and novels which are today, along with the War works, most identified with the period. Two of the best examples of writers who used this small group of people as characters were Noel Coward and Evelyn Waugh, although there are others, such as Aldous Huxley and Beverley Nichols, who were equally famous for doing so.

The characters in Waugh's novels and Coward's plays were often rebelling against their society's conventions, not for any high goal but for their own personal pleasure,[33] usually ignoring any personal pain they might cause others along the way. One of the best examples of this quest for personal happiness of those who were close to the character can be found in Coward's play "Private Lives" [1930], which was about a divorced couple and their new spouses and their search for personal happiness at the cost of everyone else's. None of the four are willing to compromise to make the people they are supposed to love happy; that job belonged to the other person. Two short examples show the attitude assumed by the young quartet.

Elyot	"You mustn't be serious, my dear one, it's just what they want."
Amanda	"Who's they?"
Elyot	"All the future moralists who try to make life unbearable. Laugh at them. Be flippant. Laugh at everything, all their sacred shibboleths.
Amanda	"It was chance meeting you. It was chance falling in love; it's chance that we're here, particularly after your driving. Everything that happens is chance." [34]

And, it must be added, it was chance that put the divorced couple and their new spouses in adjoining hotel rooms with a shared balcony, allowing the divorced couple to meet and fall in love again. All of the four demand that the others fall in with what would make that individual happy. This narcissism is also prominent in many of Coward's other interwar works. In some, such as "Design for Living" [1933] and "Hay Fever" [1925], it was the main cause of the action.

Many of Coward's plays were hits when they were first produced, and most reflect the attitudes of their period fairly well. Not all of Coward's plays have to do with selfish young couples or other manifestations of the Bright Young People. Two of his plays were about the effects of the Great War on British society. One of the plays, "Post-Mortem" [1930], was a failure, while the other, "Cavalcade" [1931], was one of Coward's biggest hits. The contrast in the way the two plays present the pain of the Great War may help in understanding British feelings towards the War as postwar turned into prewar.

"Post-Mortem" is the story of how John Cavan, a young officer killed in the spring of 1917, sees the future of his loved ones in 1930 as he lay dying in the trenches. The best adjective to describe this play is vitriolic. The scenes in the trenches could have been written by Sherriff or Aldington, and Cavan's speech to his friend Perry—

> "Look here, Perry, I've been here longer than you and I'm going to give you some advice whether you like it or not. You're heading for a smash.... [W]hatever it is, shut it off, keep it down, crush it! We can none of us afford a personal view out here, we're not strong enough—no one is strong enough" [35]

—could have been written by Graves. If Coward was correct when he analyzed his feelings towards the War, which were quoted near the start of this chapter, then it can only be supposed that he found a profound understanding of the warriors' literature.

In any event, Cavan visits his future, hoping to find if his statement to Perry ["Somebody must be learning something from all this." [36]] has come true. Instead, he finds that he could not have misplaced his hopes more. His fiancee has become merely a character from "Private Lives," and her last speech seems meant to sum up the experiences of those women who had lost their lifes' mates during the War, and had to make do in the shallow lonely years afterwards.

> "Don't be miserable, please—if you'd come back all right years ago and we'd married as we'd planned, it might have been different.... [Y]ou

died young, who are you to judge, you who hadn't
found out about everything being a bore."[37]

While the scene between John and his tabloid-owning father borders on high comedy, the most moving scenes are the ones between
Cavan and his poet friend Perry and the one with the other officers of his
unit. In reply to Cavan's desperate question "Why so bad? What is it?
What's happening?", Perry replies with a long speech which shows a disillusionment which could be thought of as typical of the idealistic officer
who found that the Great War to end war and reform the world had in
reality done nothing but waste the things which were important to
him.[38] Perry then commits suicide, after thanking John for his visit.

How some of the warriors have slipped, forgetting what war was
really like, is shown in the scene where Cavan meets the other three
officers who were present at his death. Coward describes them in the
stage directions as having "somehow less life in them than there was
when they were together in War,"[39] and they are to be played by different actors. All three men have buried the War as best they could: the
traditional "young" officer ["Babe"] has almost forgotten the memory of
his hero, a slightly older officer who died offstage just as the play was
beginning, and he seems slightly shell-shocked. John believes that
perhaps "life hasn't compensated him enough for not dying."[40] The
jokester of the group, Shaw, on the other hand, has gone solemn and
patriotic, and the type who might have been called a Colonel Blimp in a
few years' time.

Shaw	"If I had sons, and there were a war, I'd shoot them if they didn't go.... Because I don't believe in shirking one's responsibilities."
John	"To what would your sons be responsible?"...
Shaw	"I'd bring them up to believe in God, and the necessity of standing by their country in time of need, and to play the game according to the rules." [41]

Shaw had become, in short, the embodiment of the public school code and the playing fields of Eton. Neither Shaw nor Babe will allow themselves to remember the horrors, experiences, or fears the War caused, any more than they would remember the dreams and hopes they thought they had been fighting for. Tilley, their commanding officer, accepted his experiences, but was trying to minimize the whole era: "I accept life and peace, as I accepted death and war. They're equal as jobs, and I'm a worker.... I'm passing the time...just passing the time."[42] Tilley does not, however, make a convincing stoic.

Nowhere does Cavan find what he has looking for–a reason to live. The postwar world has turned out to be everything he did not want it to be, and his major hope for that postwar world, that something good should come out of all the pain and sacrifice of the War, is the least true of all. Cavan's findings about the future are summed up in his final words at the end of the play, as he is once again back in the trenches: "you were right, Perry–a poor joke."[43]

"Cavalcade" was an even greater success than "Post-Mortem" was a failure. Like "Post-Mortem," "Cavalcade" is in general about the War, and is very difficult to describe, as it covers some 30 years in 21 scenes. At first reading, it is easy to see how "Cavalcade" gained its reputation as a patriotic play. Through all the tribulations which the upper class couple endure between 1899 and 1930, they always manage to keep their love of Britain. The love of country starts the play, as the young Robert volunteers for the Boer War, and ends the play, when Robert and his wife toast in 1930.

Jane	"What toast have you in mind for tonight—something gay and original I hope?"
Robert	"Just our old friend—the future. The future of England...."
Jane	"Now, then let's couple the future of England with the past of England. The glories and victories and triumphs that are over, too." [44]

If anybody missed the theme of patriotism during the bulk of the play, it ends with a spotlighted Union Jack and the singing of "God Save the King" to drive the point home. The real point of the play, however, is not so much the couple's love of England, but what they had to endure during the years the play took place. This theme is presented by the rest of Jane's toast.

"Let's drink to your sons who made part of the pattern and to our hearts that died with them...and

let's drink to the hope that one day this country of
ours, which we love so much, will find dignity and
greatness and peace again." [45]

Like the patriotic sentiment being echoed by the singing of "God Save
the King," the negative side is also portrayed by the song which
immediately precedes it: the "Twentieth Century Blues."[46]

Coward wrote of "Post-Mortem"

> I wrote an angry little vilification of war called
> "Post-Mortem," my mind was strongly effected by
> Journey's End, and I had read several current war
> novels one after the other. I wrote "Post-Mortem"
> with the utmost sincerity.... In fact, I tore my
> emotions to shreds over it.... There is...some of the
> best writing I've ever done in it, also some of the
> worst.... I might have done better had I given I
> given more time to it and less vehemence. [47]

If the section of Coward's autobiography which concern's "Cavalcade" is read[48] with the above passage in mind, there can be no doubt
that "Cavalcade" was meant to represent many of the same feelings as
"Post-Mortem." But where John Cavan found nothing worth surviving for
in the Britain of 1930, Jane and Robert Marryot at least keep the hope
of a better future going. Unfortunately, Coward may have succeeded so
well in disguising the underlying meanings of the play that "Cavalcade"
will remain only a patriotic play,[49] as even Coward was forced to admit.

> Everyone seemed to be more concerned with
> "Cavalcade" as a patriotic appeal than as a play....
> I hadn't written the play as a dashing patriotic
> appeal at all.... The irony of the war scenes had
> been missed by the critics—naturally.... [50]

One social historian was probably correct when she said that "Cavalcade" "had caught the mood of the people and put it in focus,"[51] even if that was not Coward's hope or intention. As Coward states,[52] the fact that "Cavalcade" opened just before the very emotional 1931 National election, seemed to fit right in with the calls for doctors' mandates for the Government and the theme of national unity.

Coward was by age as well as at least partially by experience a member of the wartime generation. The postwar generation quickly produced equals to the two civilian writers of the war generation who were famous exponents of disillusionment in their writing [Coward and Huxley] in Evelyn Waugh and Beverley Nichols [who is dealt with in a different context in the next chapter]. After Coward, it is to Waugh that many critics look to for characters who fit into the general definition of "Bright," especially in his first two novels, Decline and Fall [1928] and Vile Bodies [1930], although the first is more an attack on British "smart" society in general, while the second deals more with the Bright people.

It is interesting to note, although it was probably no more than a coincidence, that these first two novels, attacking upper-class British behavior, occur almost like bookends to the great upsurge of the warriors' literature. There can be no doubt that Waugh had little sympathy for the leaders of the warrior writers, at least at the time.

Some of Waugh's writing clearly shows that while the warriors were trying to find their youth, which they had sacrificed to the War, Waugh was trying to push them aside in favor of those who were truly young:[53]

> I hope that I shall not be thought ungrateful to the men who defended me when I was a helpless schoolboy in the O.T.C. if I mention the fact that once again there is a younger generation. [54]

The main cause of this attack on the warriors may be seen in the first sentence in the above quote—Waugh <u>was</u> being "ungrateful," and in other essays from the 1920s, Waugh shows his feelings about having not been old enough to participate in the Great War. These feelings showed themselves in two basic ways: the first, putting down that "older generation" of warriors; the second, a lament that he had not been, and probably would never become, a warrior himself.

This second theme is easily found in any collection of Waugh's writings from the interwar period, especially in the 1920s.

> You know, Bill, what we want is another war....
> [W]e have a great body of young men...just longing for another general disturbance....
> We also know that when there is a war the fighting people at least have moments of really intense enjoyment and really intense misery.... [55]

Waugh repeated the first sentiment in his most famous work, <u>Brideshead Revisited</u>, which was written during the Second World War, when he has the narrator, Charles Ryder, say in the early 1920s:

> It's rather sad to think that whatever happens you
> and I can never possible get involved in a war. [56]

It is the second half of the theme, however, that gets the most play–the idea that his generation was brought up in the atmosphere of war, and that this was therefore their natural element. Waugh made this observation often in the essays,[57] and perhaps explains this passage in Brideshead:

> It seems to me that I grew younger daily with each
> adult habit that I acquired. I had lived a only
> childhood and a boyhood straitened by war and
> overshadowed by bereavement...that summer term
> ...it seemed as though I was being vain a brief
> spell of what I had never known, a happy
> childhood.... [58]

Waugh presents the view that his generation was in competition with its older brothers, a competition which Waugh and his friends could not win for two reasons: the first, because they could never outdo their elders in valor [since it was believed–or hoped–that war was outlawed]; second, because their older brothers maintained their claim on youth. At least some of the disillusionment which the Bright Young People felt, according to Waugh's literary evidence, may be traced to guilt at having avoided the War, and resentment towards those of their elders who had fought.

Waugh's way of dealing with this jealousy of the warriors was through insult and satire towards the warriors and glorification of those his own age. Waugh started his buildup of his generation at the expense of the warriors as early as 1921, in an article called "Too Young at Forty."[59]

Waugh's main satire of the warriors, which goes along with the ideas expressed in the above-mentioned essay, was the character of Captain Grimes in Waugh's first novel, <u>Decline and Fall</u>. On the surface, Grimes appears to be a typical warrior officer: gruff; missing a leg; and a Public School Man. In reality, he is an alcoholic and a bigamist, who had been kicked out of both Harrow and the Army, and who lost his leg when he "was run over by a tram in Stoke-on-Trent," although he maintains the fiction of having lost it during the War.[60] Grimes survived because of his title of captain and because he had been to Harrow. His long speech on the subject was meant to show that those who had been to public schools <u>and</u> had been officers in the Great War would always be favored over others.

> "[Y]ou see, I'm a public-school man. That means everything....
> 'God bless my soul,' (said the judge), 'if it isn't Grimes.... What's all this nonsense....' So I told him. 'H'm,' he said, 'pretty bad. Still, it's out of the question to shoot an Old Harrovian....' And next day I was sent to Ireland...." [61]

Grimes is everything that a man of his position and social and military background was not supposed to be. He is also, as Waugh called him, "of the immortals."[62] Grimes is not, of course, supposed to be the typical of the warriors, even though he is their only representative in the novel. He is, however, a symbol of the network which kept public school officers employed in the hard times of the 1920s. Dorothy L. Sayers' character George Fentiman in The Unpleasantness at the Bellona Club[63] found work in much the same way. For the young men of Waugh's age, it must have been galling to see these men given innumerable chances while they, products of the same social system and of the same caste, were kept out because they had been too young to have fought in the War.

Some of those of Waugh's generation did go the warriors one better in one area, however. They took the warriors' cynicism and quest for eternal youth [the warriors would have been in their early thirties to mid-forties at this time for the most part] a step further. Instead of being cynical about their world, they tried to ignore it, and concentrated on being young, rather than just acting young. Unlike the warriors, the poor, the proto-feminists, and most of the other people discussed in this chapter, these very young people were not disillusioned because of their experiences and the problems which surrounded them, they were disillusioned with themselves. They were "bored at twenty," feeling that the only thing left to rebel against were "the widest conceptions of mere decency."[64] The War was supposed to reform society, anything which it had not reformed was therefore probably unreformable, at least by any individual or group, especially at a time when upper-class power and privilege were in retreat. If, during the 1920s, the Edwardian period was seen as the golden sunset of an age, the 1920s were often seen as an interlude between the War and the final disintegration of civilization. This sense of "the Fall of the West" could only be encouraged by the coming of the worldwide depression and the shadow of another war. It is in this context, feeling blocked off from the past by the War, from success in the present by those who had fought in it and general economic hard times, and afraid of what the future might [and did] bring, that the actions and feelings of the Bright Young People and the characters in many of Coward's plays and Waugh's novels can be understood.

There is one other body of evidence which could be brought forward to show the discontentment the upper classes felt during the inter-war years: travel literature. While it may seen strange to put the idea of travel into the same category as the warriors' literature, the Bright Young People, etc., travel was the one manifestation which linked the disillusioned upper classes together besides their class. Not all the disillusioned were scarred warriors, and even fewer were Bright Young Things, nor were they all disenchanted with the idea of life itself. All these people, however, seem to have wanted to be somewhere other than where they were. In fact, in a small way, this idea of travel even transcended class, as many members of the working classes [at least those who were employed] found they could travel at least once a year or so for mere pleasure, even if it was only from London to Blackpool or Brighton.

The best overall analysis of interwar British travel is Paul Fussell's Abroad,[65] subtitled "British Literary Traveling Between the Wars." Although it mainly deals with travel literature written in Britain between the wars, it is, in many ways, a sequel to Fussell's earlier work <u>The Great War and Modern Memory</u>.

As Fussell points out, the need many of the warriors felt to travel was a natural outgrowth from their experiences during the War. Guy Chapman, one of the literary warriors mentioned in the first chapter, agreed with Fussell's assessment, at least where he was concerned: "I suppose there is something absurd about the intense happiness I get out of the simplest travel abroad.... I must say I enjoy being alive."[66] These sentiments are complimented by the statement of a private quoted by Fussell: "We thought that after the war we would quit the monotonous life at home and we would go adventuring."[67] For men trapped in the cold, damp trenches, daydreams of sun-drenched beaches might help them get through the days,[68] and the same could be said for those in dreary, ration-conscious Britain.[69] Once the War was over, one thing that most people seem to have agreed upon was a need for change, even if some felt the change should lead backwards. For many of those who felt the need for change, it was easier to change the setting of their lives than to change the social, political, and economic environment of Britain. And, as Fussell points out, even if radical changes were made to the above factors, it still could not help Britain's weather.[70]

For whatever reasons, the British travelled like never before during the interwar period, especially during the 1920s. Fussell was undoubtedly deliberately overstating the case when he suggested that the reason so many people left Britain was because of a "conviction that Britain is uninhabitable because it is not abroad."[71] Nevertheless, the cult of travel during the 1920s was symptomatic of the disenchantment

many Britons felt about their society. Sayers, who tried so hard to cap-
ture the times she was writing about, has her hero Lord Peter Wimsey
travel not just the usual spots, such as Rome, Paris, and the French
countryside, but the United States, Corsica, Spain, and the Basque
areas. Wimsey was, after all, as disillusioned as any Noel Coward
character, and much of the travel literature reflects the disillusionment
of the period as well as the Wimsey series, the Coward plays, etc.

The subsection of the travel literature which fits best into the theme
of disillusionment would not be the thinly disguised adventure literature
as much as the stories of travelers who managed to escape from the
confines of Britain and British society. While these travelers always had
at least as many problems as those who had remained behind in the
Home Counties, their problems had the advantage of being different.
While those at home often felt they were watching the "Decline of the
West" there, they felt they could still be like the explorers of old, if they
could ever get abroad, and those who travelled, or lived, abroad could
be seen as superior because of the "daring" needed to break loose. A.
J. P. Taylor, as usual, made similar conclusions some twenty years ago:

> The writers with a meaning conveyed a doleful
> lesson. Nearly all turned against their age and
> repudiated it as far as they could. They were
> expatriates in spirit and usually in place as well....
> These interwar writers present a puzzle to the
> historian. Literature...reflects contemporary life
> and reveals its spirit. To judge from all leading
> writers, the barbarians were breaking in....
> Civilized men could only lament and withdraw, as
> the writers did to their considerable profit. [72]

The reasons Taylor found this attitude to be puzzling seems to be twofold: 1) he cannot imagine why the material improvement of the post-war years did not bring universal happiness to those who enjoyed it [Taylor claims that the 1920s were "the best time mankind, or at any rate Englishmen, had known....."[73]]; and 2) he never connected the many strains of disillusionment which he comments on through his works together. For Taylor, the expatriates were those who went off to live in Paris, the deep countryside, or the United States, or perhaps those who joined the Catholic Church or became saved through communism and the class struggle. The many who tried to escape through the reading of the travel books, the many mystery and adventure stories, the fantasy lands of the movies or radio, are ignored. Taylor even fails to tie in the many economic ills which he can describe so well to the disillusionment of anyone.

The key word which Taylor never found which helps explain the many faces of the 1920s is "escape." There were so many reasons to feel uncertain throughout the interwar period: economic problems and the many social problems which went with it [mass unemployment, strikes, and during the early part of the era, the fear of revolution]; the changing social values of British society and the problems of adjustment to those changing values; and, of course, the many social, personal, and political problems caused by the War. While the War was over, and supposedly won, the great losses and uncertain postwar settlement mocked the ideas of a great victory and a lasting peace. The lasting effects of the War on the minds of so many of the British people, and the threat of future war, made a return to Victorian optimism difficult for many.

With hope for the future barred for many, at least along conventional routes, perhaps escapism in British society, in all its forms, should have been expected. Some, as recorded by Fussell, escaped abroad, others escaped through time [as did Robert Graves, through his historical novels], others through religion [such as Waugh, who converted to Catholicism], or through fantasy. And, of course, as mentioned above, many times the above number escaped by reading the literature produced by those who did escape, as well as through the new mediums of radio and the movies.

Perhaps a partial explanation of the discontent of the interwar period was given by Freud in his aptly named 1930 work, <u>Civilization and its Discontents</u>.

> The question of the purpose of human life has been raised countless times; it has never yet received a satisfactory answer and perhaps does not admit of one....
>
> We will therefore turn to the less ambitious question of what men themselves show by their behavior to be the purpose and intentions of their lives.... The answer to this can hardly be in doubt. They strive after happiness; they want to become happy and to remain so....
>
> As regards...the social source of suffering...we do not admit at all; we cannot see why the regulations made by ourselves should not...be a protection and a benefit for everyone of us. [74]

People were not happy in interwar Britain, as the brief, and incomplete, mentions of the social and economic problems in this chapter should have indicated. As time went on, especially after 1931, a new problem was added to the question of disillusionment: the problem of war, until it at least came close to equalling the economic problems for the common people. To be more specific, the new questions were when the next world war would come; would it be truly the war to end all wars, but in the sense that civilization would not survive it?

The public had, of course, been told that the Great War was to be the last war—no more world wars, or general European wars; no more colonial wars; no more minor wars in far-off countries between people the British knew little about; no more civil wars which might draw in other countries. People wanted to believe it. Some people had to believe it. Not everyone could believe it, however—and as time went by, it became harder and harder for anyone to believe that peace [at least peace for Britain] was possible.

The idea of the next world war is not often directly mentioned in the contemporary social histories [or political histories], although the idea is often skirted in a variety of ways. In fact, if only the formal social, political, and intellectual histories are read, one could be excused for believing that only a few people on either end of the political scale were aware that even the possibility of another world war could occur, and that those very few in between who felt it was possible [even if it would mean the end of civilization, and what sane country's leaders would wish to end civilization?] believed that organizations such as the League of Nations Union would solve the problem.

There are other references, however. Some were as simple as John Cavan's remark in "Post-Mortem:" "There'll always be another war."[75]   Other examples are more complex, or at least more extensive, such as the epilogue in Evelyn Waugh's second novel, <u>Vile Bodies</u> [1930], which is set during a short lull on "the biggest battlefield in the history of the world."[76]   The literature and general essays of the inter-war period are sprinkled with these examples, although they seem to increase dramatically as the 1930s continued, and by the time of Munich they were quite common.   The change over from pacifism in reaction to the Great War to alarmism over the character of the next war can best be seen in the life of one of the "bright" authors of the 1920s, Beverley Nichols.   Nichols, who had been the darling of the pacifists when he wrote an exposé of the armaments industry called <u>Cry Havoc!</u> [1933] changed his opinion over the necessity of war when it came to defending Britain in his <u>News of England</u> [1938], as explained in the next chapter.

A more common source of this theme of referring to the next war was combined with the travel book.   Nichols wrote such a book in 1936 called <u>No Place Like Home</u>, and Douglas Reed combined the above two genre's with his memoirs of the Great War in <u>Insanity Fair</u> [1938].   Two of the best examples, though, are Rupert Croft-Cooke's <u>The Man on Europe Street</u> [1938] and Philip Gibbs' <u>European Journey</u> [1934].   Although Croft-Cooke's work is at times more entertaining, and, since he was not nearly as well known, it is slightly more believable that the common people [or, as he would have said, his neighbors on Europe Street] would have talked to him, as he rode around Europe in his converted bus, than to Gibbs in his chauffeured car.   Gibbs' work, however, is the more valuable historically, having been written so much earlier. It is also interesting to note that both men claim the same conclusions about the popularity of having to fight another war: very few people, even the Germans, wanted even a minor war in Europe. Everyone seems, however, to fear another war by accident.[77]

Another point in common between Croft-Cooke's work and Gibbs' is the assumption of internationalism on the part of Europeans. The thing which made both their trips possible was not the mere geographic fact that it was possible to drive around Europe, but the underlying assumption that all Europeans [including the British] had enough in common to allow free communication between the travelers and the people they meet along the way. This idea of internationalism was going against the nationalist trend of the entire interwar period. On the most practical level, this nationalism could be found, for the traveler, in the new passport regulations, which meant, for the first time in generations, the frontiers of Europe could be closed to individuals in peacetime.[78] It was to see how much this nationalism affected the people of Europe in their daily lives, to see how much the political nationalism of the 1930s was the nationalism of the people, that these two writers went on their trips.

One thing was clear to Gibbs as he made his way through Europe during the spring and summer of 1934: the type of internationalism which was symbolized by the League of Nations did not have many adherents. The feelings the common people had about the League, as Gibbs found them, is best shown in the scene Gibbs set with a group of workers in front of the uncompleted Palace of the League of Nations in Geneva:

> "We're not building a new palace for the League
> .... [It's] a new hospital for the wounded of the
> next war."
> "I know what I'm helping to build.... This, mon-
> sieur, is a barracks we are building. It will be
> ready for occupation by the Germans when they
> march this way ...."
> Perhaps they took us for three...delegates to the
> Disarmament Conference....
> It was worth all our journey to hear those words. [79]

In his introduction, Gibbs stated that he believed that the common people of Europe whom he had seen

> looked out on life with shrewd eyes. They were
> realists.... They were able to express their ideas,
> their fears, their bitterness... with remarkable
> clarity and gift of speech. [80]

What Gibbs heard mostly, though, was confusion. The people he talked to saw the problems caused by the world wide depression, the build-up of arms throughout Europe, and realized that they had no idea what the future might hold.[81] As Gibbs summed up: "We had found that fear of the future was the dominate thought in this anxious Europe of 1934."[82] That the leaders of the British Government could maintain their optimism in the face of the many reports which filtered through to Britain was amazing.

The war so many people feared was not, in many ways, as bad as the war which occurred. Yet with such a major catastrophe as the Great

War burned into everybody's mind, an even worse war, such as the one in H. G. Wells' 1933 novel <u>The Shape of Things to Come</u>,[83] could not be considered mere fantasy. Against the growing fear of another world war, one which promised to be much worse than the last, the British public put its faith in the League of Nations and a group of policies which were supposed to go with the League. The two major policies in this group being collective security and disarmament.

The League of Nations was many things to many different people and groups. It may even be argued that the League might have prevented the Second World War, may have even been the last chance the world had for something approaching world peace, had the politicians really believed in its ideals and had the general public better known its limitations. Instead of being the semi-supranational body which it could have been [and was occasionally believed to have been in popular mythology and the political rhetoric of the time], the League was only at best a mere debating society, whose main accomplishments were not its various attempts to bring about world peace and universal disarmament, but the more mundane achievements of international copyright codes and regulations against the so-called white-slave trade.[84] In retrospect, it is difficult to believe that it was not realized that the League of Nations was powerless to stop international aggression unless its member nations, especially Britain and France, were willing to take certain risks to promote peace. Yet all evidence points to the fact that most people believed [or wished to believe] that the existence of the League was enough in itself to stop aggression. The problem of this split between belief and fact is shown by the following two passages found in Donald

S. Birn's The League of Nations Union.

> During the 1935 General Election [Harold Nicol-
> son] received a letter from a constituent asking for
> an assurance that Nicolson stood for the League
> and collective security and that he would 'oppose
> any entanglements in Europe.' Nicolson de-
> scribed how he read the letter aloud at various
> meetings and observed the response. 'Only in rare
> and isolated cases,' he recounted, 'did my audi-
> ence at once see that the above formula was...
> contradictory nonsense.'

> The League of Nations Union cannot be held ac-
> countable for the failures of the 1930s, then, but it
> can be faulted for the notions the public had
> about the League. Cecil admitted that he should
> have emphasized in the early days that if you
> wanted peace, you must be prepared to fight for
> it. The LNU did not offer the kind of rigorous
> critique of the League...mechanism or of the prin-
> ciple of collective security that might have
> equipped the British public to face the...1930s with
> a sober, realistic perspective. [85]

However, there was really almost no critique of the League until

after the war which the League had been set up to prevent was in pro-

gress. As the possibility of another world war turned into actuality as the

1930s progressed, more and more of those who had worked throughout

the interwar period for permanent peace joined the multitudes of others

who had become disillusioned since 1914. It is impossible to know why

so many people had come to the conclusion that pacifism in some form was the answer to the world's international problems, especially when coupled with a powerless debating society and vague notions about the power of world opinion. And, according to Joyce Berkman, "[f]ew pacifists were aware consistently of...pacifist premises,"[86] and that "pacifist conviction derived often from nontangible influences."[87] The pacifism of many Britons, although perhaps not of the pacifist leaders, disappeared in 1938, after the German takeover of Austria and the subsequent war scare in the late spring.

Of course, much of the evidence of interwar opinions and sentiment were never set down and are now lost. The reasons why most of those who had been working for various pacifist causes, the League, the Peace Pledge Union, etc., lost heart and gave up rather than making a greater effort in 1938 and 1939 are now lost. The loss of support, both financial and of volunteers, were recorded in the various pacifist journals.[88] After Munich, but before the invasion of Czechoslovakia, the pacifist groups seem to have accepted the fact that there would soon be another war, as they moved away from attempts to promote international good will and turned instead to the formation of anticonscription groups and research into methods of draft-dodging.[89] In a sense, the disillusionment of the British people was now complete. Those fired by idealism had now joined the many others who had hoped for a better world and who had believed in the promises given during the Great War.

About the only group of people who were not disillusioned during the winter of 1938-39 was the British government and its followers. The British needed peace to recover from the many shocks it had received from 1914 onwards, and the National Government had promised peace.

These policies of peace are known today under the blanket term of "appeasement."

NOTES

1. Noel Coward, <u>Present Indicative</u> [New York, 1937], pp. 101-102.

2. Coward only spent a short time in the army, first of all because he was too young to volunteer had he wanted to, and also too young to be drafted, as he was born in 1899; secondly, because his health quickly broke down once he had been drafted. <u>Ibid.</u>, pp. 73-87.

3. <u>Present Indicative</u>, p. 102.

4. Both the so-called "Wars of the Roses" [itself a 19th century term], and the English Civil War were romanticized out of recognition, although not as much as the Hundred Years War had been, by 1914. The American Revolution was either regarded as the defeat of a bad king [and therefore acceptable] or a minor setback in what could almost be termed the Second Hundred Years War, which started against Louis XIV and included the victories of Marlborough, and ended with the wars against Napoleon. The mess of the Crimean War was lost in the legend of Florence Nightingale and the heroism of the Charge of the Light Brigade [which, along with the evacuation of Dunkirk during the Second World War, is a perfect example of this process]. To finish off the process, by showing it was active in the late Victorian age, the death of Gordon was seen as glorious and a prelude to the conquest of the Sudan, and Churchill's exploits in South Africa distracted the British public, to some extent, from the type of war being fought there. It seems a well-known quirk of the English to love some of their defeats as much as their victories.

5. George Dangerfield, <u>The Strange Death of Liberal England</u> [New York, 1935].

6. Wohl, pp. 113, 121, 203-237. Other tallies are even higher.

7. The coalition consisted of 484 MPs: 338 Conservative; 136 Lloyd George Liberals; 10 others. Against this large majority were 59

Labour, 26 Asquith Liberals, 48 Conservatives, 4 Independents, and 7 Irish. 73 Sinn Feiners were elected, but did not participate. Mowat, pp. 6-7.

8.	For a brief account of Britain's early recession, see Mowat, pp. 25-36.

9.	Labour was in as the minority Government in 1924 and 1929-1931. The Conservative had majority rule in their own right 1922 through the end of 1923, and 1924-1929, and were the majority party in Parliament throughout the rest of this period.

10.	Mowat, pp. 6-7, 145, 167-168, 187-190, 350-352, 409-412, 553-555.

11.	The only general interwar election which was fought on a specific issue was the 1923 election over tariffs, and that election was one of the two [out of five] that Baldwin lost.

12.	Taylor, 1914-45, pp. 115-116. Before the war there were about 7,000,000 voters, the new law added 13,000,000 more males and 8,500,000 females to the roles. The residence requirement excluded 5% of the voters in any given election.

13.	Ibid., p. 94. Graves made the comment that "the Great War...freed the Englishwoman." Week-end, p. 39. See also Stevenson, pp. 82-85.

14.	Taylor, 1914-45, p. 38.

15.	Ibid., p. 38. See also Sheila Rowbotham's Hidden From History [London, 1973], p. 110. She covers women and the War pp. 108-122, and interwar Britain, pp. 123-166.

16.	For an example from literature, see the exchanges in Strong Poison between the head clerk and Miss Murchinson.

17.	Week-end, pp. 36-50, 99-112; John Collier and Ian Lang, Just the Other Day [New York, 1932], p. 131; and David Low's The Best of Low [London, 1930], p. 35.

18.	Week-end, p. 44. For another Sayers reference, see the confession of the culprit in Gaudy Night.

19. The term could mean anything from the "problem" of women entering the workplace, to women getting degrees at Oxford, to the problem of women so outnumbering men, etc.

20. This control did little to limit profits, however.

21. Stevenson, p. 195-196.

22. For some accounts of the General Strike, see Mowat, pp. 285-335; Week-end, pp. 150-170.

23. See the previous note, as well as the shorter references in the other interwar histories. The General Strike has also generated its own historiography, which is too complex to be gone into here.

24. Mowat, pp. 126, 165, 273-275, 357, 379, 432-433, 464-467, 469.

25. That is, those people who came from families which had been "gentile" before the war, but whose income was destroyed by the war [through lost investments in Russia, for example] or wiped out through bad investments or by the inflation which occurred during the war [the income having been derived from fixed rate investments].

26. The Bright Young People were either too young to have been in the war or did not see active service, were very well off and from upperclass families, and dedicated to having a good time while the new post-war freedom and remains of the prewar class structure existed. By the early 1930s, the few remaining young things had degenerated into the type depicted in Murder Must Advertise.

27. Stella Margetson, The Long Party [Farnborough, 1974], p. 50.

28. Other Day, pp. 121-148. Also pp. 22-40.

29. Ibid., pp. 134-136.

30. Week-end, p. 128. The first quote is from the 1925 novel Gifts of Sheba by W. L. George, the second from a 1925 article in the Daily Express.

31. Mowat, p. 214.

32. Stevenson, however, dismissed them in one short sentence about the "gay young things" [p. 240].

33. Waugh explains this near the end of his first novel, Decline and Fall [Boston, 1928], pp. 281-283.

34. This first quote is Noel Coward, Plays Two [London, 1979], p. 56. the second, p. 15. See also Leo's speech on chance in "Design for Living" in Plays Three, pp. 28-29.

35. Plays Two, p. 287.

36. Ibid., p. 286.

37. Ibid., pp. 318-319.

38. Ibid., pp. 328-329.

39. Ibid., p. 351.

40. Ibid., p. 356.

41. Ibid., p. 355.

42. Ibid., p. 357.

43. Ibid., p. 361.

44. Plays Three, pp. 196-197.

45. Ibid., p. 197.

46. Ibid., p. 198.

47. Present Indicative, pp. 334-335.

48. Ibid., pp. 339, 353, 355-357.

49. Week-end, pp. 296-297; Taylor, 1914-45, p. 314; Margetson, pp. 119, 178-179.

50. Present Indicative, p. 352.

51. Margetson, p. 179.

52. Present Indicative, p. 352.

53. The closeness of the warriors and what Waugh called "a younger generation" is best illustrated in Waugh's own family. Waugh was born in 1903, while his warrior/writer brother Alec was born in 1898.

54. Evelyn Waugh, "Too Young at Forty" [1929] in A little Order [London, 1977], pp. 7-8.

55. Ibid., "Oxford and the Next War," p. 4. The letter was written in 1924.

56. Evelyn Waugh, Brideshead Revisited [Boston, 1945], p. 101.

57. Waugh's best development of this theme can be found in Order, p. 11.

58. Brideshead, pp. 44-45.

59. Order, p. 2.

60. Decline, p. 28.

61. Ibid., pp. 31-33.

62. Ibid., p. 269.

63. Bellona Club, p. 71.

64. Order, p. 12.

65. Paul Fussel, Abroad [Oxford, 1980].

66. Ibid., p. 8.

67. Ibid., p. 9.

68. Ibid., pp. 3-8.

69. Ibid., pp. 9-13.

70. Ibid., pp. 21-23.

71. Ibid., p. 15.

72. Taylor, 1914-45, pp. 179-180.

73. Ibid., p. 180

74. The first two paragraphs are Sigmund Freud, Civilization and Its Discontents [New York, 1961], pp. 23-24; the last, p. 36.

75. Plays Two, p. 355.

76. Evelyn Waugh, Vile Bodies [Boston, 1930], p. 314. This section is on pp. 314-321. For just one additional example out of many possible novels, see the passing remarks in The Search by C. P. Snow [New York, 1934], pp. 45-56.

77. Philip Gibbs, European Journey [Garden City, 1934], pp. 24-25, 32-33, 51, 62-63, 96-97, 106-107, 189-191, 235-237, 240-246, 254-258, 264, 336-342.

78. See Abroad, pp. 24-36, for two interesting chapters on the interwar perceptions of passports and frontiers.

79. Gibbs, pp. 106-107.

80. Ibid., p. 2.

81. In just one chapter [on Italy], this feeling was expressed at least five times [pp. 139, 173-175, 178-178, 182, 185-186].

82. Ibid., p. 329.

83. The idea of a "next war" is not only found in passing references in many of the interwar novels, but also in a number of works which dealt exclusively with this topic besides Wells' now famous work. In fact, as one writer on the subject noted "...eschatological fictions in which man literally destroys his own civilization, species, or planet ...come along only in the 1890s, and there are not many of those.... But after 1914 man-made dooms are the rule...." W. Warren Wagar, Terminal Visions [Bloomington, 1982], p. 108.

84. Waugh satirized this in many parts of Decline and Fall.

144

85. Donald S. Birn, The League of Nations Union 1918-1945 [Oxford, 1981], p. 229. For another view of why the League failed, see Beverley Nichols' Cry Havoc! [London, 1933], pp. 123-124.

86. Berkman, p. 338.

87. Ibid., p. 339.

88. That is, a run of such journals from early 1938 through 1939, such as the Peace Pledge Union's Peace News or even The New Statesman and Nation. No figures are given, and is difficult to prove.

89. The National Peace Council, Peace Year Book 1939 [London, 1939], bibliography.

BEVERLEY NICHOLS–A CASE STUDY

In the last chapter, a number of different authors, and how they reflected the interwar period, were surveyed. It is time to look at a single author, his effect on public opinion and its effect on him, in a little more depth. After all, the appeasers themselves, both at the time and in their memoirs, claimed that appeasement was in large part forced upon them by public opinion, citing as proof such events as the "Oxford Resolution," the East Fulham by-election, and the Peace Ballot. One problem with all these instances is that they all occurred before both the 1935 general election and most of the events which are directly linked with the policies of appeasement [e.g., the reoccupation of the Rhineland, the Abyssinian Crises, the Anschluss, Munich, etc.].

During the years 1935-1939, as international events pointed more and more towards the possibility of war, the leaders of the National Government also blamed two general political movements in Britain for their own slowness in rearmament and their lack of vigorous protest of German and Italian aggression: the British Labour Party and the pacifist and anti-war movements. The fact that the Treasury and Neville Chamberlain had long before decided that rearmament on a Churchillian scale was both impossible and unnecessary was never publicly discussed.[1]

146

Unfortunately for the appeasers, as many later historians have noted, it was at this time that moderate members of the Parliamentary Labour Party very slowly started turning away from the traditional Labour policy of disarmament, towards a policy of limited rearmament and calls for British action against fascist aggression, especially in Spain. It was also the time when the British pacifist movement was losing its membership, as the pacifist organizations stopped promoting world peace and disarmament through the League of Nations to the extent they had during the early 1930s, and instead began gearing up to help those who might wish to become conscientious objectors in the war most of them feared was fast approaching.[2]

Even though none of the evidence which the appeasers put forth for showing that their policies holds up,[3] there is equally no convincing evidence that appeasement was either popular or unpopular with the mass of Britons. The modern opinion ion poll was just starting in Britain during the 1930s, and was mostly confined to product research. Newspaper columns, letters to editors and MPs, accounts from Mass Observation, etc., are all interesting, but they cannot provide any positive proof about how the British public felt or reacted towards the events of the 1930s and have even less to show about how those opinions might have changed during the decade.

Yet if mass opinion is almost impossible to guess, individuals can be accessible. Changes in the opinions of individuals may be even easier to find if that person was a "private citizen," and so could more easily adapt his/her opinion to events, rather than a public official or politician, who might have felt some compulsion to follow a "party line."

One well-known individual who wrote on the topics of pacifism and the international situation during the 1930s was the popular novelist Beverley Nichols, who is often lumped together with writers like his contemporary Evelyn Waugh.[4] Nichols is important because, in addition to being a novelist, he was also identified with the pacifist movement during the early 1930s. Therefore, Nichols' famous pacifist work shall be described before outlining some of the changes in his thinking during the 1930s, and finishing with suggestions on how those changes might influence the ongoing study of appeasement.

Nichols' most famous pacifist work was the non-fiction British best seller of 1933, Cry Havoc!, dedicated by Nichols "TO THOSE MOTHERS WHOSE SONS ARE STILL ALIVE." Havoc! was, first and foremost, an attack on the international armaments industry. It was also, however, an apology for the pacifist and anti-war movements. Havoc! is never, on the other hand, an appeal to the logic of the British people. It instead tried to make an emotional impact on the reader, while always staying within the bounds of reason. Therefore, although much of the book deals with the international armaments industry and its believed danger to international peace [along the same lines of the well-known 1934 American book, Merchants of Death[5]] Nichols also used much of the remaining space in Havoc! to describ the types of weapons which might be used in the next European war, and their effects on the general population.

The greatest fear of the interwar period was aerial bombing with high explosives along with what was simply called "poison gas," which included both chemical and biological weapons. This general fear finally became expressed with the simple phrase, "the bomber will always get through." Nichols therefore concentrated on what he believed would happen to the great cities of Britain once those feared waves of unstoppable bombers "got through."

For the modern reader, it might be difficult to realize that Nichols was talking about the effects of twin-engine bombers dropping high explosives and some poison gas, since much of his rhetoric sounds more like the effects of a limited nuclear strike rather than the type of air raid possible during the early 1930s.[6] Nichols never the less spent a great deal of space in Havoc! trying to show that the statement "the bomber will always get through" was a self-evident fact, rather than a truism, as well as the "fact" that many of those bombers would be dropping poison gas.[7] With these facts "proven," at least as far as he was concerned, Nichols could then devote himself to explaining how various poison gasses affected people, concluding that portion of the book with a brilliant chapter on what life wearing a gas mask would be like, based on his own research in a gas mask factory.[8] Nichols devoted remaining portion of the book was mainly devoted to general anti-militaristic propaganda.

Of course it is impossible to know just how influential any given work might have been. Joyce Berkman, in her 1967 dissertation "Pacifism in England: 1914-1939," called Cry Havoc!

> ...a singular influence...in addition to its own particular data and deductions, it summed up and advertised the conclusions of pamphlets and books of [pacifist] literature. Lastly, the author and his book captured and reflected to an unusual extent the spirit of the times. [9]

Even if <u>Cry Havoc!</u> was not as important a work as Berkman and others, including this author, believe it was, it certainly did mirror that section of British public opinion which swelled the ranks of the pacifist movement in the early-to-mid 1930s. Nichols' bald statement that "no great city can be defended the air, and therefore from gas attacks"[10] had been well-known in some form for years, appearing in the popular press and in the pronouncements of the self-proclaimed military experts. The sentiment would gain even greater circulation after Stanley Baldwin gave it its most famous and final form, "The bomber will always get through,"[11] and find its greatest literary expression in H. G. Wells' <u>The Shape of Things to Come</u>, which was of course turned into the popular movie "Things to Come." <u>Cry Havoc!</u> came near the beginning of a series of events linked to this concept of danger from the air joineded to pacifism [or at least anti-militarism],[12] and must be seen as at least a typical product of the mentalité in Britain during the early 1930s, even if it should someday be shown not to have been one of the pivotal works from that period, as is now generally accepted.

The importance of Nichols to the study of appeasement, however, does not lie in <u>Cry Havoc!</u> itself, or in any of the other related minor works of Nichols from the early 1930s.[13] Nor does it lie in some of Nichols' oft-repeated statements, such as:

> ...I publicly proclaim...my desire to be shot in the nearest backyard, within twenty-four hours of the declaration of war, rather than shoot, or gas, or drown, or otherwise murder any of my fellow men. If a man makes that statement...it is presumed that he will either have to stand by it...or else be

> denounced as such a hypocrite and a coward that
> life will be unendurable for him. [14]

Instead, Nichols is important because he did not stand by his pacifist statements as the 1930s progressed, and he made his new opinions as public as he had his former pacifist ones. Why did Nichols change his views, and how did he escape being called a "hypocrite and a coward?"

In his 1949 autobiography, All I Could Never Be, Nichols claimed that he had never really been a sincere pacifist at all. Rather, he had only been caught up in the swelling public movement against militarism, and had written Cry Havoc! in order to capitalize on that prevailing public mood.[15] While Nichols may have been telling the whole truth in 1949, it does not explain away all his other pacifist writings of the early 1930s. It is at least as possible that Nichols' 1949 claim was also at least in part a capitulation to the then prevailing public sentiment against the pacifism of the early 1930s which occurred after World War II.

How then did Nichols' opinions change, and why did they do so? There can be no doubt that Nichols had greatly changed those pacifist views he had expressed in Havoc! by the time he started writing News of England, subtitled A Country Without a Hero, in the autumn of 1937.

Where Cry Havoc! was mainly concerned with the various aspects of militarism and pacifism, News of England is concerned with various aspects of social and political life in Britain in 1937 and early 1938. The primary theme seems to have started out being how Nichols understood the changes in the international situation since 1933, how those changes had affected Britain, and the prospects for further change in the near future.

However, Nichols was at the same time also trying to understand the apparent fact that most people in Britain seemingly either had no idea about what was going on around them in Britain and Europe, or just did not care about what was going on. In fact, although the main theme of the book starts off being an examination of the growing dangers of the international situation, by the end of the finished book the moral decline and fall of the British Empire and the English race become equally important themes. Therefore, the book itself is awkwardly split, with some sections dealing with international concerns and others with the internal decline of the English people—with only occasional attempts to combine the two themes.

While the sections dealing with Nichols' sardonic search to find a "hero for modern England" are certainly of interest to the social historian, they must be left out of this study. Instead, the more obvious parallels between Cry Havoc! and News of England will be discussed. Nichols went on at fairly considerable length in Havoc! in telling his readers what the possible effects of bombing a major city could be, especially if some of the bombs contained poisoned gas. Much of the pacifist literature from the interwar period also made mention of those believed consequences, as did both popular literature and the popular press.[16] Whatever power the pacifist movement had during the interwar period—especially during the 1930s—should be attributed in large part to the shock this type of literature and writings caused amongst the general public.[17]

152

So, in 1937, Nichols went looking to see what effect all this literature and information had had on the British public and their institutions. He was shocked to find out that all this information had really had no effect on the Britain of 1937. Nichols' favorite example seems to have been the Brighton Town Council's dicussions of air-raid exercises:

> [O]ne of the most distinguished members of the Town Council felt bitterly aggrieved.... He said:
> "It is outrageous that Brighton should be the one sea-side place to start frightening away its visitors by having a blackout."
> To which another Town Councilor...added a loud 'Hear, hear'.... [18]

Nichols spent an entire chapter expressing his amazement that, as far as he could tell, the vast majority of the British population was "sound asleep" when it came to the possibilities of a new general war in Europe. As Nichols saw the danger of war increase between 1933 and 1938, it became impossible for him to understand why the majority of his fellow citizens were not making as much noise about it as he was. To the man who had painted gory pictures about what life during an air attack, especially without a gas mask, might be like, receiving a letter which stated:

> [i]f any nosey young official came round to my door, and told me to put on a gas mask (which I regard as the invention of the devil), I'd slam the door in his face, and if necessary go to prison before I'd wear it.... [19]

could only make Nichols wonder what kind of country he was living in during the latter 1930s.

Where in 1933 Nichols had feared that a general European war might be caused by what would now be called the "military industrial complex," by the winter of 1937-1938, as he came to believe that war with the Fascist powers was inevitable, Nichols did not even mention his earlier fears of the international armaments industry in News of England, let alone blame it in any way for the state of Europe. Also in 1933, Nichols believed that the League of Nations might yet bring about a new and better international order, and used an entire chapter in Havoc! to outline the various possibilities.[20] In News of England, Nichols could hardly say enough negative things about the League and its role in international affairs as it existed in 1937-1938. Where in Havoc! it was only the selfish actions of nationalistic politicians which Nichols saw as being the only problem area for the League,[21] by the time Nichols wrote News of England, he was classifying the entire League system as a danger to European peace.

> It is necessary to insist, ad nauseam, on the lunacy of a pro-League policy .... long after the League has ceased to exist. It is necessary for the simple reason that...the British people are sunk in such apathy and indifference that they do not appear to realize it.... Nor do we appear to mind.... [22]

In News of England, Nichols did not really renounce the majority of the opinions that he published in Cry Havoc!, or at least he did not admit

154

to having renounced them. Instead, Nichols claimed that it was the world which had changed by that winter of 1937-1938, and Nichols, who had once stated that

> ...I am as fluid as water...my family motto is
> 'Anything For a Quiet Time,' emblazoned under...
> an excessively 'couchant' lamb .... [23]

flowed right along with the changing times, much to the dismay of the many pacifists who had admired <u>Cry Havoc!</u> and Nichols' other pacifist works from the early 1930s.

Nichols portrayed himself in both works as a man in search of knowledge, a man looking for the best answers to the questions of war and peace, who was bringing the reader along on the journey. To Nichols in the early 1930s, the most probable causes of war were the international armaments industry and those nationalists and militarists who were perhaps too willing to use the arms provided the various nation-states, and the refusal of the leaders of those nation-states to work together. Nichols saw the dangers, and presented them to the European and American public in the belief that once the people knew about the dangers, and saw them as Nichols saw them, those dangers might be negated. At the same time, Nichols saw two possible routes to future peace: pacifism and the League of Nations.

Unlike some pro-League propagandists, Nichols did not see the League of Nations as the possible cure-all for international troubles. Rather Nichols believed that the League could become the basis for a true supranational organization. While Nichols, unlike some of the

League's more enthusiastic supporters, realized that the greatest threat to the operation of the League came from the national [and nationalistic] leaders in every member country, he still believed in 1933 that it was possible for those leaders to rise above mere nationalistic goals.

By the time he wrote News of England, however, Nichols had come to realize that the national leaders of the League's member countries were unable to rise above national goals, although he still seems unable to believe that such action on their part was impossible. Nichols seems shocked to have discovered that politicians were still treating the League "as a reality" when he could only see a "phantom" of its promise of 1933,[24] apparently unaware that for those politicians, a phantom was all the reality the League was ever supposed to have had.

In any event, whatever possibilities existed for the League in 1933, whether in reality or just in Nichols' mind, they had been destroyed by 1937 by the debacle of the disarmament conference and the international antics of Germany, Japan, and above all, Italy,[25] along with the French and British reactions to those activities. In the wake of his dis-illusionment, Nichols turned on the internationalism which he had once championed as ideal as well as necessary, just as he did the organization of the League itself.[26]

Yet what about Nichols' famous statement, that he would rather be shot than be forced to "murder" fellow citizens of the world? While Nichols tried to explain in large sections of News of England why he had lost his faith in the League and internationalism, why the British people should still wake up and look for the bombers, and why the international

156

situation was so much worse in the early spring of 1938 than it had been in 1933, etc., how did Nichols finally justify his change of heart?

"Finally" is the correct word, because Nichols did not address these questions until the last chapter in <u>News of England</u>. It was only here that Nichols mentioned <u>Cry Havoc!</u> And it is only here that Nichols tried to explain his new outlook.

> Five years ago...in a world where there was still hope for the League, still hope for disarmament... <u>Cry Havoc!</u> was timely....
> All the same, I could not write <u>Cry Havoc!</u> to-day. It would be like waving a fan in a cloud of poison-gas.
> The profound loathing and horror of war which made me write that book is...stronger in me than ever.... war settles nothing. For every problem it solves, it creates a hundred new problems. [27]

If war is still so terrible in Nichols' mind, then what could possibly ever justify war? And, if war can ever be justified, something Nichols did not believe possible in 1933, what did he now believe about pacifism?

> And yet I believe that there are some things worth fighting for. To this 'loathsome necessity'... have I come, in company with a large number of pacifists. I do not see why we should be ashamed of of ourselves. We have not been inconsistant. We do not pretend that war is anything but legal-ized murder. But we do at least see that some-thing very precious may vanish altogether from the world unless we are prepared to defend it. And that something is the English spirit. [28]

And so, by the spring of 1938, Nichols had abandoned whatever pacifistic views he had ever held. Anyone ready to defend the British Empire by the sword cannot at the same time agree with the statement, as Nichols did in <u>Cry Havoc!</u>, "I would rather suffer death unjustly than to take life in a just cause,"[29] or with the answer to the question posed a few pages later in that same book: "Wouldn't you use a revolver on your fellow men in any circumstances?" "No."[30]

By the spring of 1938, Nichols had found what he believed was a "just cause" for taking life, and a circumstance in which he, at least, would use a revolver.

While it would be possible, and certainly interesting, to trace the growing patriotic and imperialistic sentiment in Nichols' writing between 1933 and 1938,[31] that search lays outside the scope of this study. Instead, the fact that Nichols did change from one of the better-known popularizers of the anti-war movement into a defender of the "English spirit" and the British Empire must be dealt with in reference to the larger theme of appeasement studies.

Why might a person, who was important in pacifistic and anti-war circles, renounce his opinions? Nichols certainly was not a left-wing political activist, or for that matter a left-wing anything, as his references to the British Empire and the chapter in <u>News of England</u> entitled "A Study in Red"[32] easily demonstrate. Nichols himself only said that it was the changing world around him which made him change his opinions, or, as he would have probably preferred to have phrased it, modify his opinions to meet a new set of facts. Nichols never went into detail on how or why those opinions changed, preferring to let the readers make their own judgments.

It could actually be that in many ways Nichols really was "as fluid as water" in his opinions, and did change his opinions as those who were around him and those he wrote for changed or modified their opinions as events warranted. If this is true, then Nichols' basic statement on why his opinions changed holds true, and no further explanation is needed. It raises, however, the greater and more important question of why all these other people changed their opinions on the relative merits of pacifism and the need of having a real defense and the will to use it, a question to be addressed in the next chapter.

If, like Nichols, part of the anti-war and pacifist movements were moving away from their goals and ideals of the early 1930s towards the view that Britain needed a stronger defense, and many of the remaining pacifists were giving up the struggle to prevent rearmament in order to prepare help for conscientious objectors, where were all those pacifists that the leaders of the National Government claimed stood in their political way of pressing rearmament forward between 1936 and 1938? As Berkman remarked:

> By 1938 it was clear that the pacifist movement had lost momentum...existint aims and proposals [were] diluted...or simply elaborated.... The only chance pacifists had to exert direct influence on government policy was lost in 1935.... [33]

The reason why Nichols is important to the study of appeasement is not because he was always so accurate either in his facts or in his predictions [he was not], nor because his opinions directly mirrored either those of the British public in general or even of the English educated classes [none of which could ever be proven true or false]. Neither is Nichols just important because he helps show what historians of appeasement have often stated but never really proven–that the appeasers given reasons for appeasement [public pressure] were declining as the international situation worsened, and appeasement became more blatant.

Rather Nichols' works give the historian an idea of the broader range of opinions which were present in Britain during the 1930s, and how far and fast opinions could change. It is very easy to limit the discussion of appeasement and general British foreign policy to the appeasers, the Labour Party, the Churchillians, and the extreme pacifists, and ever more detailed studies by later historians. A broader picture of the intellectual and popular opinion matrix which existed in Britain during the 1930s is needed before a more accurate account of why there was appeasement, and why the British public reacted to it as it did, is possible. In such a study, individuals such as Beverley Nichols are a good place to start looking for the reactions of the British public.

NOTES

1. Robert Paul Shay Jr., <u>British Rearmament in the Thirties</u> [Princeton, 1977], pp. 32-37. See the discussion of Shay in the next chapter.

2. Berkman, pp. 309-16.

3. See the penultimate chapter for a discussion of these arguments.

4. Nichols was a year older than Waugh, and also went to Oxford in the early 1920s, where he was president of the Oxford Union. He became well known in the mid and later 1920s for his satiric novels and his narcissistic autobiography, <u>Twenty-five</u>.

5. H.C. Engelbrecht and F.C. Hanighen, <u>Merchants of Death</u> [New York, 1934], which cites Nichols.

6. In general, nearly every writer during the interwar period greatly overestimated the amount of damage which could be caused by the conventional bombing possible during the interwar period, or even that possible during World War II, to the point where even a few bombers were thought able to produce as much destruction [leaving aside the affects of radiation] as a modern atomic weapon!

7. <u>Havoc!</u>, pp. 60-70.

8. <u>Ibid.</u>, pp. 70-84.

9. Berkman, p. 174. Although it is rarely cited, Berkman's work seems to be the best secondary source on interwar British pacifism, especially in its literary aspects.

10. <u>Havoc!</u>, p. 74.

11. Shay, p. 37; also Kenneth Rose, <u>King George V</u> [New York, 1984], p. 386.

12. For details on this type of literature, especially the fiction, see Wagar, pp. 108, 124.

13. Such as Nichols' play <u>Avalanche</u> [1932], <u>For Adults Only</u>, his apologia for pacifism in general [London, 1932], and the many varied articles Nichols wrote during this period.

14. <u>Havoc!</u>, p. 10.

15. Beverley Nichols, <u>All I Could Never Be</u> [London, 1949], p. 212.

16. Mowat, pp. 537-538.

17. Berkman, pp. 169-185.

18. Beverley Nichols, <u>News of England</u> [London, 1938], p. 43. The section on Brighton covers pp. 41-44.

19. <u>Ibid</u>., p. 48.

20. <u>Havoc!</u>, pp. 143-154.

21. <u>Ibid</u>., pp. 145, 147, 151-154.

22. <u>News</u>, p. 19. See also pp. 15-24.

23. Beverley Nichols, <u>No Place Like Home</u> [London, 1936], p. 37.

24. <u>News</u>, pp. 15, 19.

25. <u>Ibid</u>., pp. 16-18.

26. <u>Ibid</u>., p. 30.

27. <u>Ibid</u>., pp. 305-06.

28. <u>Ibid</u>., pp. 306-307.

29. <u>Havoc!</u>, p. 182.

30. <u>Ibid</u>., pp. 185, 189.

31. Nichols' love of England, especially his "own" little piece of it, can especially found in his travel book <u>No Place Like Home</u>. See pp. 316-318 for the most obvious example.

32. <u>News</u>, pp. 115-132.

162

33. Berkman, p. 311.

BRITISH FOREIGN POLICY & APPEASEMENT

> We cannot tell whether Hitler will be the man who
> will once again let loose upon the world another
> war in which civilization will irretrievably succumb,
> or whether he will go down in history as the man
> who restored honour and peace of mind to the
> great German nation and brought it back serene,
> helpful and strong, to the forefront of the
> European family circle.... It is enough to say that
> both possibilities are open at the present moment. [1]

If Winston Churchill could publish the above statement in 1935, it
should not be surprising that other British leaders [perhaps with less
imagination than Churchill] were also uncertain about what to make of
the new German leader. The Second World War and the atrocities which
followed appeasement are both so terrible and so very well-known that
it is difficult to recapture a view of the events of the 1930s without this
'afterview' coming into play. These last two chapters, however, will make
an attempt.

So far the world-view of disillusionment has been shown in some
of its many forms, especially those connected with the effects of the
Great War on the minds of members of the British public. In the final
chapter, how those leaders may have used that world-view to meet their
own programs will be examined. Before that can be done, however, the
general foreign policy problems of the 1930s must be examined.

In August 1931, economic problems caused by the worldwide depression led the leader of the Labour Government, Ramsey MacDonald, to try and form a National Government of all parties. For a variety of reasons, most of the Labour MPs refused to follow their leader, and the official Labour Party was badly beaten in the next election.[2] Despite the fact that the Conservative Party was the majority party in the new Parliament, MacDonald [who had acted as his own Foreign Secretary in the First Labour Government and tried to hold the same jobs in the second] remained as Prime Minister, and the-then Liberal Sir John Simon was named Foreign Secretary. Both MacDonald's new National Labour Party and the Liberal Party[3] were pledged in some degree to the ideals of collective security, the League of Nations, and disarmament. In spite of the many changes of circumstances [and even Parliamentary membership] and another election, the National Government would last until May 1940, and would claim to support the policy of collective security, the League, and disarmament in some form until the spring of 1939—even though the actions of the National Government were mostly against those ideas after 1935. It is the tragedy of the National Government that it was formed in 1931 to meet economic problems, but was forced to deal with foreign problems which was outside its ken, and that of most of the general public as well.

> At the time [1931-35], men blinked at the mounting difficulties of the Disarmament conference and at the great debate whether peace could be preserved by means of the League of Nations. Foreign affairs were all along the interest

of a minority. For most men, economic questions came first, and foreign policy was debated in such moments as could be spared from wrangles over unemployment. The government were content to have balanced the budget.... [4]

In retrospect, it is easy to see that two of the major foreign policy problems that British leaders should have faced up to in the early and mid-1930s were the threat of Japanese expansion and the fact of German rearmament. But when the British leaders spared foreign policy a passing thought, imperial concerns loomed larger than any foreign threat.

Although many of the inter-empire problems of the so-called white dominions[5] were solved by the 1931 Statute of Westminster, there still remained problems in Ireland and India, as well as a dream called Imperial Preference. Even if all three were to some degree important questions, they loomed in the forefront of foreign affairs because of the political passions and memories they aroused, rather than the absolute merits of the arguments made about them, or because they were the most important non-domestic questions the British had to face in the 1930s. For example, the Irish used the Statute of Westminster to make themselves independent in all but name, and these actions resulted in a short but bitter trade war between the Irish and the British, proving the old rule "that English statesmen took leave of their senses when dealing with Ireland."[6] Despite the fact that the issues which caused the trade war and which were caused by the trade war were solved–at least to the satisfaction of the governments of the day–the British leaders believed they had to treat the Irish problems with great care, if only because of the historic passions and problems Irish policies had caused in the recent past.

Like the problems with Ireland, India and Imperial Preference caused a great deal of pother in British political circles, but presented problems without any real dangers. Imperial Preference was an attempt to create a customs union throughout the British Empire, especially between the Dominions and Britain. The leaders of the National Government supported the idea because the Dominions had very high custom barriers, and if the leaders of the Dominions could be persuaded into lowering tariffs for British goods, those goods would have an advantage over non-imperial goods and be better able to compete with the domestic products of the Dominions. This could only help the failing British export market and help bring Britain out of the Depression. The ideas of Empire Free Trade [which never had a real chance] and Imperial Preference were destroyed at the Ottawa Conference in 1932, although some tariffs were raised for a few non-imperial goods [leaving British products still at a disadvantage against domestic Dominion goods]. The difference was not enough to help British industry, and the National Government was forced to look inward to try and solve Britain's economic problems. The failure of the Ottawa Conference, from the British point of view, helped to discredit MacDonald and allowed the Conservatives to push through the end of free trade in Britain. This forced most of the mainstream and left Liberals out of the National Government. As these Liberals also formed the left wing of the Government, the National Government became even more dominated by the Conservative Party and its two main leaders, Stanley Baldwin and his second in command, Neville Chamberlain.

The changing status of the Indian Empire ended the short term influence of the main political power in the middle of British Politics. When the British viceroy, Lord Irwin [later the Earl of Halifax] announced, without prior permission, in October, 1929, that India would someday receive full Dominion status, it was in effect all over bar the timing. Churchill, who deeply believed in the British Empire, tried to use the Indian issue to take over the Conservative Party in 1931. This attempt to break Baldwin's hold on the Conservative Party cost Churchill a post in the National Government, any immediate chance of the Conservative leadership, and much of his influence in Parliament.

The threefold problems of Imperial Preference, Irish irritations, and the dominion status of India may seem trivial compared to the great foreign policy issues of the 1930s, such as disarmament in the early 1930s, and the threats to peace after 1934. In fact, the first two turned out to be largely irrelevant, while the final outcome of the third was settled except for the details in 1929. Of course, it would take twenty years to work those details out.

These three issues, however, occupied the available time for foreign policy to the near exclusion of other topics between 1931 and 1935.[7] While the National Government was spending so much of what little time it spent on non-internal problems on these issues, the policies which had been touchstones for all three major parties in 1931 were being turned into mere shibboleths by circumstances by 1935. Whatever potential collective security through the League of Nations, the Kellogg-

Briand pact to outlaw war, and the goal of universal disarmament may have had for succeeding 1931, they were near impossible goals by 1935; that was the year the British leadership realized it had to put foreign policy on at least a near par with domestic issues.[8] Unfortunately, collective security, the League, and disarmament remained the avowed goals of the Labour Party and the claimed ideals of the National Government right through 1939.

In the 1920s, the only nations which could even come close to challenging Britain militarily were France, the United States, and Japan; the first an ally, the other two former allies and believed close friends. With no potential enemies in sight, there is little reason to wonder at the low military budgets and the adoption of the so-called ten year rule.[9] All three branches of the military were allowed to deteriorate far below the minimum standards needed to protect the Empire.[10] Not un-naturally, the military suffered even more during the early stages of the Depression because of the conservative-style budget slashing by the-then Labour Chancellor of the Exchequer, Philip Snowden [who remained Chancellor during the four-month First National Government], and also by the man who would be Chancellor for the following five and a half years, Neville Chamberlain. The 1932 military budget was the lowest of the interwar years,[11] and the next two only slightly better.

While the military continued to deteriorate, the National Government started on its confused two-way course in foreign policy. On the one hand, it repealed the ten year rule in 1932 and made plans to strengthen the port of Singapore, as well as allowing the military Staffs a wide range of planning initiatives. On the other hand, the military budgets were kept very small and some effort was put into the Disarmament Conference in Geneva.

The Disarmament Conference was supposed to put teeth into the Kellogg-Briand pact, turn the war machines of the world into international police forces, and insure that the international status quo was not changed by violence. Instead, the years of the Disarmament Conference [1932-33] saw the end of the postwar era and the start of the prewar.

> It was hard not to conclude that the disarmament conference was rather a mockery, as Secretary Stimson said, when the opening of the conference, on February 2, 1932, was delayed for an hour or so that the League council could discuss the bombs falling on the helpless population of Shanghai. [12]

The Conference, if it did not start out as a mockery, soon became one as the cause of disarmament was buried in the political struggles of the major powers. The two main problem areas were the conflict between German calls of equality between all nations [meaning allowing Germany to rearm, or, according to the Germans, the disarmament of everyone else] and the French claim that an armed France and a disarmed Germany was the best insurance of peace, and the Anglo-American attempt to replace true disarmament with the reduction of only "offensive" weapons. This attempt led one of the U. S. delegates, Senator Claude Swanson, to become immortalized

170

> sitting in the Sea Commission, blowing great
> clouds of smoke from his cigar and demonstrating
> in fervid Southern eloquence that battleships were
> the most defensive of weapons; they became a
> symbol of the American home and family, they
> could be given to children to play with as toys, so
> harmless was their use and purpose. [13]

Although other delegates rarely used such interesting metaphors, they were, for the most part, just as interested in having the Conference fail in its purpose as the Southern senator. When the conference adjourned in December 1932, it had accomplished very little. The 1933 sessions would merely be stages for the Nazis, until Hitler withdrew his delegation from the Conference and the League on October 14, 1933. Any hope for disarmament should have ended by October 1933, if not a year before. Yet the National Government leaders would continue to invoke the spirit of disarmament while disobeying the letter [although usually in the most moderate ways] throughout the 1930s, and most members of the Labour Party would protest against rearmament during the same period, even when demanding armed intervention in Spain or protesting the growing power of Hitler.

Another hope which refused to die was collective security, operating through the League of Nations. Just how collective security was supposed to work was unknown in 1931. The first real test was the Japanese invasion and occupation of Manchuria in September, 1931. Japan had broken the Kellogg-Briand pact, the Washington treaties, and the Covenant of the League of Nations. The question was what the Great

Powers and the League were willing to do to help China. The answer, in effect, was nothing. It was not in the interests of any of the Great Powers to try and force Japan to back down,[14] and the League could not act unless at least one of the Great Powers was willing to take the lead. Instead, the League set up a commission of enquiry, under Lord Lytton.

And so, in the end, none of the Great Powers or the League did anything that affected the Japanese conquest of Manchuria. The Japanese puppet state of Manchukuo was not recognized, but that did not affect Japanese control in any way. Economic sanctions were talked about, and mechanisms for boycotts were set up, but not used. More importantly, Japan was forced out of the League and set out to arm as fast as possible.

Taylor, in his famous Origins of the Second World War, states that the Manchurian affair has often been overrated by those who claim that it was the end of the possibility of collective security, preferring to reserve the failure of the Disarmament Conference for that role. In fact, Taylor believes that the Manchurian affair has drawn far too much attention: "The Manchurian affair had a contemporary importance, though not that subsequently attributed to it."[15]

It must be pointed out, however, that Manchuria had many parallels with the Italian conquest of Abyssinia, at least as far as the League was concerned in each one. If Taylor was correct when he said of British attitudes towards the League in 1931–"[t]he British had always regarded the League as an instrument of conciliation, not a machine of security"[16] –then either the British Government changed its collective mind by the time of the Abyssinian Crisis four years later, or it was acting during that Crisis with little faith or belief in the methods being used. It is also possible that the course of events which the League followed, at British suggestion, in 1935 was almost predestined by the events of the Manchurian affair, including the nonrecognition of the Italian conquest and the use of the boycott machinery which the League had set up in response to the Japanese conquest. It would have taken real initiative for the British and French leaders not to fall into the trap of precedence in dealing with the Abyssinian Crisis, and neither set of leaders had any.

After 1933, events started to move quickly, or at least too quickly for the leaders of the National Government to stay head of them. 1934 could have been a decisive year had the National Government acted according to its knowledge, for that was the year in which the need for rearmament was acknowledged and the policy for rearmament for the next six years set. The policy makers realized by that time that both Germany and Japan were possible threats to British security, which was a major step for them. The only real decision made about how to deal with this possible double threat was the decision that Britain was not powerful enough to fight both powers. This decision, which would affect British foreign and military policies for the next six years, was not made by the Prime Minister, or the leader of the largest party in the National Government, or by any other minister. It was made for the political leaders by the civil servants of the Treasury, and none of the leaders of the Government really fought that policy during the following six years.

> The Treasury argument...was that because the nation lacked the resources to engage two first-class powers simultaneously, it had to decide which was the more serious threat and concentrate its resources on meeting it while trying to accommodate the other. [17]

And so the Treasury's assessment of Britain's power, and the willingness of the leaders of the National Government to accept the Treasury's assessment, required that a policy of appeasement for either Germany or Japan from the outset. Germany was considered the greater threat, if for no other reason that while Japan threatened the entire Eastern Empire [Hong Kong, New Zealand, Australia, and even India], Germany threatened Britain. In addition, Germany was only starting to rearm, and it might be easier to match Germany than Japan. Under the pressing problem of how to react to the possible German threat [still seen only as possible, not definite], MacDonald and Baldwin referred the problems to various committees for further study.[18]

The perfect solution for Britain—according to Neville Chamberlain—can be considered an early version of what is now known as the nuclear strategy of Mutually Assured Destruction [MAD], then known as the "knockout blow" those few times it was named. The great fear in this pre-nuclear age was the bombing of civilian targets, possibly with poison gas, which would cause a great deal of destruction and panic. Again, the belief was that "the bomber will always get through."[19] This belief in the all powerful bomber allowed Chamberlain and others to believe that if any service should be built up, it should be the R.A.F. [which also

happened to be the least expensive to improve—on paper]. Later on
however, the expensive bombers were scrapped for cheaper fighters
one instance in which the Treasury did make the correct decision for the
politicians, even if for the wrong reasons.

The problem of air power was brought out in a House of Commons
debate in November 1934, when Churchill announced that the German
air force would soon be more powerful than the British. Answering for
the Government, Baldwin responded with platitudes and a vague
promise in his penultimate paragraph to "bring his [Churchill's] request
to the notice of the Prime Minister."[20] Perhaps as the result of
Churchill's badgering, a few weeks later Baldwin made his infamous
promise that

> this Government will see to it that in air strength...
> this country shall no longer be in a position infer-
> ior to any country within striking distance of our
> shores. [21]

The debate which emerged over the R.A.F. had many ramifications.
First of all, it gave the R.A.F. a great deal of political clout when it was
dealing with the Treasury; unfortunately, that meant that any increases
approved for the R.A.F. would usually come out of the army budget, not
that the overall military budget would increase faster than the Treasury
and Chamberlain deemed "safe" for the national economy.[22] Also, although in the short run the promises gave assurances of future British
power, it also exposed for the more knowledgeable Britain's military
weaknesses over the years 1935-42.

In short, Britain's military weaknesses and unwillingness to quickly
earm because of the poor health of the economy led to a "catch-22" situation. Britain could protect its interests, and itself, especially in the
short term, only through some form of collective security or alliance sys-
em. Britain's weaknesses, however, caused doubt both overseas and
at home about how much Britain could contribute, or would be willing to
contribute, to any security arrangement. Why should any nation ally
itself with Britain if Britain could not, or would not, be of assistance if
needed?

This was the main flaw with the entire idea of collective security as
it was usually understood in the interwar period. The political left in
Britain wanted collective security within the framework of the League of
Nations, and insisted that it could be accomplished with a minimum
amount of armaments, being against the manufacture of arms [especially
for profit] on principle, and also because a minimum of arms would cur-
ail imperialist adventuring. Collective security could come into being,
however, only if Britain and/or France had the power and the will to be
able to take any first or quick steps by themselves. Other nations had
little desire to act as surrogates for the Great Powers. The British and
French leaders showed the depths of their political will, intelligence, and
courage twice in the years 1935-36. The Abyssinian and Rhineland
crises showed that these leaders lacked all three qualities.

The Italian/Abyssinian problem might have been as successfully ignored as the Manchurian affair had it not been for a number of circumstances which were by themselves trivial when compared to the fact that
one nation was trying to conquer another. The fact that Italy and

Abyssinia were both members of the League should not have mattered since both China and Japan had also been members in 1931; it was more the hypocrisy involved that upset the British, since Italy had sponsored Abyssinia's membership in 1923 over British objections. Japan and Manchuria were far off places to the British public; Abyssinia was close to British interests in the Middle East and East Africa, and Italy was a favorite vacation spot for the British uppercrust and a European power. Haile Selassie I was a known personality to the British through the newsreel coverage of his 1930 coronation long before he appeared at Geneva. On top of these and other trivial facts, the world had changed since 1931. The world seemed more dangerous, and so it was harder to ignore this last crisis than the first.

The British Government had to face this new crisis while they were already trying to deal with the problem of having to appease either Germany or Japan, while trying to deal with the other. Although Italy was not considered to be the equal of either Germany or Japan as a threat to worldwide British security, it could be as dangerous within the smaller theater of the Mediterranean. As Hitler was deemed to be the major possible threat to Britain, then either Mussolini would have to be appeased or the British had to run the risk of Hitler growing too powerful while they were dealing with Mussolini. There was also the possible threat of Mussolini joining Hitler, although Italian/German rivalry over Austria was thought to be too intense to allow such an alliance.

The recognized beginning of Britain's foreign affairs problems was in 1935, which was supposed to be a happy year for the British people. The country was slowly recovering from the Great Depression, a generation which had not really known the Great War was growing up, and the country was preparing to celebrate the Silver Jubilee of the beloved George V. Italy, France, and Britain had joined together at the Stresa Conference in April 1935, to warn Hitler not to change European borders by violence, and a few days later the League condemned German rearmament. A few weeks after the French and the Soviets signed a mutual aid pact on May 2, Hitler promised to abide by the Locarno treaty, and offered to sign non-aggression pacts with any European power, except the U.S.S.R. Peace and better times were thought to be in the air during the spring and early summer of 1935, and this feeling was given voice in the so-called "Peace Ballot."

The Peace Ballot, which could have easily been called the "League of Nations Ballot," showed the collective support the British people had for the League, or at least for their concept of the League. Basically, the League of Nations Union and some thirtyeight other peace and pro-League societies sponsored a very unscientific survey to find out what the British people though of certain aspects of the League and various foreign affairs issues. The most important question[23] was the final one:

5) Do you consider that, if a nation insists on attacking another, the other nations should combine to compel it to stop by:
a) economic and non-military measures?
b) if necessary, military means?

	yes	no	doubtful	abstention	Christian Pacifist
5a	10,027,608	635,078	27,255	865,107	14,121
	86.68%	5.49%	0.24%	7.48%	0.12%

5b	6,784,368	2,351,981	40,893	2,364,441	17,482	
	58.65%	20.33%	0.35%	20.44%	0.15%	[24]

The British people had showed that they supported the League and the idea of sanctions. They also supported, but less enthusiastically, the idea of using military force, a fact almost always ignored by the people at the time and later historians.[25] With an election required by November, 1936 [many leaders of the Government were hoping to call one sooner], the various Government leaders had either to rely on sanctions and persuasion to restrain Italy, or rely on their political skills and the wisdom of the electorate to save them from political defeat if military means were quickly ruled out. This meant in practice that any action which could possibly need military means as a backup would have to be ruled out as well.

And so the leaders of the National Government were trapped. On the one side, the British people supported the League, and the Press was vocal in its support: the Times; Spectator; New Statesman; and the Beaverbrook papers all lined up for the League.[26] The Government had to support the League Covenant, without using the military or even threatening to use it, or face the possible destruction of the League as any type of tool in foreign affairs and face the wrath of the British press and public just before a national election.

Mussolini was also needed by the French and British leaders to restrain Hitler in Central Europe. If opposed, Mussolini might align with Hitler, and the Stresa Front, which had seemed so powerful in the spring when the three governments had stood up to Hitler over Austria, would

:ome to nothing, and Hitler would have his first real ally. It was also possible that if France and Britain fought Italy [not a possibility talked about very much], they could become so militarily drained as to be unable to oppose Hitler, or even appease him. Finally, if defeated, Mussolini might be overthrown and replaced by a revolution. To the British Government, a Communist takeover of Italy would not be a welcome change of affairs.

Seen in the light of French and British security, the attempt to buy off Mussolini with the so-called Hoare-Laval plan made sense. It is impossible to know if Mussolini would have taken only a half of Abyssinia as offered, and it is equally impossible to guess what the reaction of the British public would have been if faced with a fait accompli. As it turned out, the French press leaked the deal before either Mussolini or the British Cabinet had heard of it. Public reaction in Britain forced Sir Samuel Hoare out of the Foreign Office, and Anthony Eden came in, although Hoare would become First Lord of the Admiralty in six months [June 1936] and would be one of Chamberlain's main advisors until Chamberlain's fall from power in 1940.

Britain now faced a hostile trio of powers. Baldwin was being urged through the more vocal press to take some type of action against Italy. If Baldwin had been the sort of Prime Minister who was able to force a point of view across without worrying about the consequences, Britain could have cut its problems by one hostile nation. Baldwin was unwilling to take a stand because he looked only at the surface facts: if Britain stopped Italian shipping to Abyssinia through the Suez Canal, Britain would probably have to fight Italy alone. Even though Britain would probably win, it would cost money, lives, and valuable ships. Also, Mussolini could fall and be replaced by something worse, in the minds of the British leaders, than fascism or Nazism–communism. The British and French Governments had already been warned by the U.S. that no interference would be tolerated with U.S. oil supplies to Italy, so the boycott of Italy that was established mostly for its public relations purpose was useful only to drive Mussolini into Hitler's camp, not to stop the Italians from finishing their military schemes.[27]

Although the Baldwin Government was embarrassed by the reaction to the Hoare-Laval plan and faced with new problems without any ideas on how to salvage the situation, Baldwin had won a large electoral victory in November 1935,[28] the month before Hoare met with Laval. The Conservative Party and National Government had far too large a majority to be shaken by the revelation of the plan–even the vote which "drove" Chamberlain from power in 1940 left him with a small but working majority despite the years of foreign policy debacles.[29] Whatever the electoral concerns Baldwin and Chamberlain had before the election should have left them afterwards. Events would show that they could force almost any policy through the Commons and were now bound to past policies only by themselves.

In theory, the foreign policy of the National Government seemed fairly simple: keeping Japan appeased and out of the British sphere of influence in the Far East; winning Mussolini back as a counterbalance to Hitler; watching Hitler and hoping power and responsibility would tame him; rebuilding Britain's defenses as quickly as sound fiscal policy would allow [but no faster]; and above all preventing Italy, Germany, and/or Japan from making any sort of common front. The attempts of the National Government to juggle these often conflicting policies have become known under the blanket term "appeasement." In the final analysis, all attempts would fail.

1936 was the year the Spanish Civil War started and Hitler ordered the occupation of the Rhineland. Along with the unfolding invasion of Abyssinia, these events, in theory, should have presented opportunities to stop the increasing power of Italy and Germany. For a variety of reasons, many of these opportunities never materialized except in myth after the fact, or were never seen at the time. The most famous example of the former is the occupation of the Rhineland.

Hitler ordered green troops into the Rhineland on March 7, 1936, confident it was a safe move. The French Government was angered by the move, but the leaders were convinced that they could not act alone,[30] which meant any action was to be determined by the British. In Baldwin's private opinion, the German move into the Rhineland was a positive move for the future peace of Britain and for Europe, since it forced France into a defensive position. This meant that the French could not launch a surprise attack on the Germans and would have to forget the idea of becoming militarily involved in Eastern Europe.[31] For Britain to become involved in a war with Germany, in Baldwin's opinion, Germany would probably have to invade France or the Low Countries. All of Eastern Europe was willingly abandoned by Baldwin over two years before Munich.

The occupation of the Rhineland has been referred to as one of the main turning points towards war, and one of the last places Hitler could have been easily stopped.[32] There are so many such turning points, however, in the historiography and mythology of appeasement, that the historian is tempted to forget them all and start over. As tempting as such a process might be, it must be resisted, and every one of the turning points must be examined, even if that examination of each point does not turn up in the written record.

While it is true that Hitler had broken the Treaty of Versailles and the Treaty of Locarno, giving the other signatories the right to clear the Rhineland of those German troops, and despite the fact that the French could have easily marched into Germany [as they had marched into the Rhineland in 1923], cleared the Rhineland, and possibly overthrown Hitler, there was no evidence at that time that this would have solved the overall problem Germany presented. In fact, while it would probably have destroyed Hitler, the European problem of Germany's activities would have been made even worse.

> The French army could march into Germany, it could exact promises of good behavior from the Germans; and then it would go away. The situation would remain the same as before, or, if anything, worse—the Germans more resentful and restless than ever. There was in fact no sense in opposing Germany until there was something solid to oppose.... Only a country which aims at victory can be threatened with defeat. [33]

In truth, the French military position was not really very much changed by the German occupation of Rhine Frontier, even though it may have been psychologically damaging to the French.

Germany's reoccupation of the Rhineland made it difficult...for France to aid her eastern allies, Poland and Czechoslovakia; in fact, she had abandoned any such idea years ago.... If the Maginot line were all it claimed to be, then her security was as great as before; if the Maginot line was no good, then France had never been secure in any case.... Germany, by reoccupying the Rhineland, used up the priceless asset which had brought her so many advantages: the asset of being disarmed. [34]

Germany had been suspected of being a possible threat to the future of European peace before the occupation of the Rhineland. Once it had been occupied by the Nazis, the German threat to European peace should have been clear to all, even if there was little or nothing which could be done about the occupation of the area itself, or even about Germany rearming. Where the talk before March was about if Germany was a possible threat, the talk afterward should have been about how to meet the German threat. Although Taylor suggests that this change in attitude did occur in some quarters,[35] there is little evidence, if any, to suggest that it occurred in the highest levels of the National Government over the next three, or even four, years. The fact, or even the probability, that Germany was a clear threat to Britain's security seems never to have penetrated to the main leaders. After all, Hitler had said after the occupation: Wir haben in Europa keine territorialen Fordernungen zu stellen [We {Germany} have no more territorial demands in Europe]; and Deutschland wird niemals den Frieden brechen [Germany will never break the peace].[36]

If it was a fact that Germany remained a possible threat to Britain in the mind of the British leaders [Chamberlain, Baldwin, Hoare, Simon, and, later, Chamberlain's aide Sir Horace Wilson] rather than a definite threat after the occupation of the Rhineland, it would explain many of the actions taken by the British Government between 1936 and 1939. An explanation of why this change in attitude failed to occur [as well as why the Labour Party leaders, who recognized the dangers to Britain, failed to act responsibly] must wait until the following chapter. A sketch of the major decisions [or indecisions] affecting the policies of appeasement should be completed.

Two "events," one before and one after Hitler's move into the Rhineland, can be pointed to show that the British attitude towards Germany did not really change because of the reoccupation of the Rhine frontier: the Anglo-German Naval Treaty of 1935 and the British Government's reactions to the Spanish Civil War, which began a year later.

On the face of it, the Anglo-German Naval Treaty was either one of the most cynical or most stupid diplomatic actions the British Government took in its relations with Germany between 1933 and 1939. Germany was "allowed" to build up to 35% of British Naval strength, including 100% in submarines. The exact reasons for negotiating the Treaty are unclear: it was negotiated during the last days of Simon's tenure at the Foreign Office but signed as one of the first acts of Hoare. Simon sidesteps the issue of the Naval Treaty in his memoirs. The closest he gets even to mentioning it was by stating his opinion of the March 1935 meeting he had with Hitler, which would lead to the negotiation of the Treaty.

> I feel no doubt that we were right to go, but I am
> equally clear that Hitler never intended to agree to
> any limitation of Germany's...designs. [37]

It is all very well for Simon, writing in the early 1950s from retirement, to be "clear" about Hitler's intentions. By the early 1950s it should have been "clear" that Hitler had been aiming for a war at some point.[38] Note the tense—Simon knew when he wrote his memoirs that he had been fooled, and tried to put the best face he could on it. Simon was honest, he could have said "was clear," but he had no excuses, no explanations and no apologies to offer, just the statement, "we were right to go."

Simon was replaced by Hoare in June 1935, when Baldwin replaced MacDonald as Prime Minister. It was up to Hoare to sign the Naval Treaty, and he did so. Hoare devotes a chapter of his memoirs of the years 1931-40 to the Naval Treaty.[39] Unfortunately, his account adds very little in understanding the reasons behind the signing of the Naval Treaty. His reasons are at best specious and/or self-deluding, at worst outright lies.[40]

Britain got no advantages out of the Treaty except the empty promise that German submarines would not attack merchant ships. The new German Navy would be much more modern than most of the British Navy and would be concentrated in the Baltic, as opposed to the British fleet, which was spread around the world. The Treaty angered both Italy and France, creating distrust amongst the Stresa Powers just before trust was needed most. Most of all, the Treaty added one more nail to the coffins of both the League of Nations and collective security, since it was a bilateral agreement which contradicted the Treaty of Versailles.

The Naval Treaty makes sense only if the leaders of the National Government either thought that Hitler could be easily bought off[41] or was not a real threat to British security, or if they were planning an alliance with Hitler as opposed to France. There is, of course, no evidence that this last idea was ever really considered.[42] In any case, the British Government also had to take Hitler at his word, and while there may have been no solid proof that Hitler was less trustworthy than any other national leader, that proof would be forthcoming the next spring. If Hitler was thought no threat or was easily bought off in 1935, why did the November 1934 directive of the Committee of Imperial Defence remain in effect?

> In November, 1934, the Committee of Imperial Defence directed those...concerned with defence...to plan on...a possible war with Germany within five years. [43]

The answer is that while war was <u>possible</u>, it was thought that it could still be avoided by good will on both sides. Germany could be appeased, if the right formula could be found. Until then, Germany could not be hampered from finding its own way. In order for it to act like a Great Power [responsibly], it had to be treated as one.

It is this attitude which explains the British response to the Spanish Civil War. The official view of the National Government, especially at first, was that the war in Spain was none of its, or anyone else's, concern.

> The first reaction of the British government–and all shades of British opinion–to the outbreak of the civil war was one of neutrality; and the policy of non-intervention was born.
>
> [T]he British government claimed to be acting solely in the interests of general peace. If all the Great Powers kept clear of Spain, the civil war could burn itself out beyond the pale of civilization.... [44]

It is quite possible, perhaps even probable, that both Hitler and Mussolini would have stayed out of Spain if the French and British had joined together and supported the Spanish Government, as the French Premier, Blum, had wanted to do.[45] It is Taylor's belief that the failure of Britain and France to support the Spanish Government which led to the drawn out Civil War, "British and French policy...not the policy of Hitler and Mussolini, decided...the Spanish Civil War."[46]

Why, then, did the British refuse to get involved, and help convince the French leaders to do the same? If one of the main goals of British foreign policy was to keep Italy and Germany from acting together, should not the British have done something positive to break them apart?

One answer is that this was what the British thought they were doing. Mussolini was still angry with the British over the sanctions issue. If it really made little difference, in the view of the British

Government, who won the Civil War, why try to stop Mussolini from aiding one side if that would make him happy? From the British point of view, nothing positive could be gained by standing in Mussolini's way. On the other hand, much might be gained by letting Mussolini [and Hitler] interfere, but keeping France and the Soviets from doing the same.

First of all, this set of circumstances should have led to a short civil war, and the shorter the Civil War, the better it would be for British investments. The fact that the Soviets [along with other outside left support] sent in enough support to enable the Loyalists to fight for three years did much to make the British leadership even more distrustful of Soviet foreign policy than they had been.

If a long war was bad for British investments and Anglo-Soviet relations, it was good for Britain's military preparedness. The British could allow the Italians to waste their resources in Spain in a war which made little difference to the British, while Britain continued slowly to rearm. This is just what happened. Mussolini committed so many men and so much material that the Nationalists were assured victory, but at the cost of eliminating Italy as a military threat, as the later Italian performances in France, the Balkans, and North Africa attest.

Neither of the British politicians concerned with foreign policy, Neville Chamberlain, the Prime Minister, or Anthony Eden, the Foreign Secretary, realized the advantages of the "long war" point of view, however, especially Chamberlain. For Chamberlain, the major British foreign policy objective for the next few years was to win Italy back as an ally. Hitler would be, to some extent, neutralized as a threat if Italy joined with Britain, France, and the Little Entente in keeping Germany out of Austria, which would have to be taken over before Hitler could hope to take any other military action.[47] An Italy friendly to Britain was therefore necessary, and if the Italian conquest of Abyssinia had to be accepted and Italian interference in Spain ignored as the price of that alliance, then that price might have to be paid.

Eden was not as simplistic in his approach to Italy. While agreeing to the need for Italian friendship in order to be able to deal with Hitler, and even willing to pay the same price to Italy as Chamberlain, Eden did not trust Mussolini to keep his side of the bargain, a mistrust perhaps based in the memory of Italy practically auctioning off its support to both sides during the First World War. Eden therefore wanted a meaningful gesture form Mussolini, such as the withdrawal of Italian troops from Spain, before the Italian conquest of Abyssinia was recognized. The value of this deal would be that of Britain and Italy would be acting as equal partners, while without it Italy could act the part of the blackmailer and continue to up the price of the alliance.

Needless to say, in the policy dispute between the Foreign Secretary and the Prime Minister, the Prime Minister won.[48] Eden resigned in February 1938, and became leader of a small group of backbenchers who were quietly hostile to the Government's policy of appeasement. He was succeeded in the Foreign Office by Lord Halifax, who had become well known for assuring the Indians that they would become a Dominion while a Parliamentary Commission was still starting to work on the political future of India–a precedence for Halifax's bowing to pressure without considering alternatives.

With Eden's resignation, appeasement entered into its more active phase, because the possibility of war now seemed more immediate. Instead of having to consider vague problems [such as how to win back Italy to prevent possible hostile German actions], the problems were at once more specific and more pressing [i.e., what to do about the German takeover of Austria].

Chamberlain had forced Eden out of office in order to facilitate a deal with Mussolini. The main reason for this was because Italy was needed, it was believed at the time, to keep Germany out of Austria, and hence out of Central and Eastern Europe. Eden resigned on February 20. By March 13, the union between Germany and Austria was a fact. Italy was then finally regarded as a true ally of Germany, even by most of the leaders of the National Government, a fact which had been true for about a year by that time. Although some attempts would still be made in the future to wean Mussolini from Hitler, the major value of an Anglo-French-Italian alliance was ended when Austria ceased to be an independent state.

It had been decided back in 1934 that Germany was the main possible threat to peace, but it was only after the occupation of Austria that the leaders of the National Government [the so-called Big Four of Chamberlain, Halifax, Simon, and Hoare, plus the former civil servant labor negotiator who had become Chamberlain's personal advisor on all matters, Sir Horace Wilson] really had to confront that threat head-on, rather than attempting to sidestep Hitler by working with Mussolini. Even though Japan remained in the background as a threat to the Empire throughout the 1930s, it was ignored in favor of concentrating first on Italy, then on Germany.[49]

The spotlight of the National Government's foreign policy therefore was finally turned where it probably should have been since 1923, or at least since 1934: Germany; not Imperial Preference, Ireland, India, or even Manchuria, Italy, Abyssinia, or Spain. The German occupation of Austria, in turn, put the spotlight on German relations with Poland and Czechoslovakia.

In the opinion of Chamberlain's close advisor, Sir Horace Wilson:

It [Czechoslovakia] was not a real country at all.
It was created out of the necessities of Versailles.
It didn't really mean a thing. [50]

Neville Chamberlain did not have a better opinion of the Czechs:

Not out of the top drawer—or even the middle.[51]

Or of Czechoslovakia:

How horrible, fantastic, incredible, it is that we should be digging trenches and trying on gas-masks here because of a quarrel in a faraway country between people of whom we know nothing.... [52]

Would the story of the Czech crisis of 1938 have been any different if Chamberlain had considered the Czechs as being out of the "top drawer"–or even the middle? Or if Czechoslovakia was considered a "real" country instead of a necessity of the previous generation of British leaders? Although it is impossible to be certain, the Czechs could hardly have fared worse in the short run.[53] Instead, it was Hitler's and Germany's needs which were considered during the Czech crisis, not those of Czechoslovakia or its citizens: Czech, Slovak, German, etc.

It appears now that Hitler did not have any "Master Plan" for taking over Europe,[54] but it can be assumed that he planned on using the German minorities in Poland, Czechoslovakia, and Lithuania to gain some territorial advantages. The real key, after the takeover of Austria, was Czechoslovakia, which had the most modern army in Europe in 1938 and a strong defensive position. Had Neville Chamberlain known something about the country, it might not have seemed so far away, and perhaps worth saving.

If the Sudetenland was truly the last territorial demand of Hitler's [with the Polish Corridor and Memel open to negotiations], then the tossing of Czechoslovakia to Germany might have ben a good power politics move, if fairly cynical even for <u>Realpolitik</u>. The larger, nineteenth-century-style Polish army was considered superior to the modern Czech, and above all Hitler was believed to be prepared for war, while Britain was still at least two years away from complete readiness. Therefore Hitler was given another chance to show himself "responsible," even though his claim on the Sudetenland was in opposition to his claim that Austria had been his last demand which could not be negotiated.

The Czech crisis of 1938 was the climax of what is now called appeasement. The policies and attitudes of the previous five years all came together to put Chamberlain and his advisors in the position of either giving in to Hitler or repudiating the policies of their Government. This would mean that three of the four National Government Foreign Secretaries would have to say that the policies they had supported and implemented [and in some cases sponsored] in relation to Germany and to a lesser extent Italy had been wrong. The foreign policies of all three Prime Ministers had been wrong. The Government policy of slow rearmament had been wrong. The attitude towards French fears of and warnings about Germany had been wrong. These errors, if admitted, could not be put down to mere miscalculation and lack of facts, as Baldwin had when he had admitted his mistake over German rearmament in the air in 1936. To have admitted such major errors would probably have meant the end of the National Government as it then existed, and possibly the end of the careers of its leaders, which for any politician would be the one thing to be avoided at all cost. According to one academic opponent of appeasement at the time, the leaders of the National Government

> really thought they were indispensable; as they looked round they could see no one fit to take their place—you can read that in their memoirs and their biographies, especially that of the self-satisfied Chamberlain. [55]

Here it should be sufficient to state that Chamberlain and his advisors stuck to their previous policies, hoping to negotiate with Hitler, and when that proved impossible, trying to get the best deal for themselves [and, they believed for Britain] rather than for the Czechs. If Hitler had kept his part of the deal,[56] Britain and its leaders would have been embarrassed but safe. Hitler did not, and the British leaders were embarrassed and unsafe, as the war in Europe started eleven months after Munich.

It is next to impossible to define and group together the foreign policies of the British Government during the 1930s. The guiding principle does not seem to have been a desire for peace as much as a great fear of war. This fear prevented the British from attempting any true disarmament when universal disarmament might have had a slight chance for success.[57] It also prevented them from using war as a threat, since war was the one thing to be avoided. It prevented both the age-old British concept of a Grand Alliance, as well as the new idea of collective security. Both pacifism and power politics were therefore impossible. Appeasement from weakness rather than from power was the only course open, other than open surrender, or as Churchill is supposed to have said:

> Grovel, grovel, grovel! First grovel to the Indians,
> then grovel to the Germans....[58]

Rowse continues the quotation with his own opinion of the leaders of the Government:

> The plain truth is that their deepest instinct was
> defeatist, their highest wisdom surrender. [59]

It is also difficult to prove that any of the leaders of the National Government were greatly affected by the disillusionment of the interwar period. They were certainly not products of it, as they were, for the most part, far too old to have been much service in the trenches. Those national leaders who had such experiences either resigned over appeasement [such as Eden and Duff Cooper], were opposed to appeasement [Macmillan and Churchill, who was in the trenches for a few months after being dismissed from office] or were on the Labour or Liberal benches. It was these older government leaders, however, who controlled the government and who made the foreign policy. It was also up to these men to sell their ideas of foreign policy to the British electorate, a great number of which were amongst the disillusioned. The interactions between the British leaders and the British public is the subject of the final chapter.

NOTES

1. Winston S. Churchill, Great Contemporaries [Chicago, 1937], p. 261. Churchill also once said of Hitler, "I admire men who stand up for their country in defeat." Quoted by William Manchester in the second volume of biography of Churchill, The Last Lion: Alone 1932-1940 [Boston, 1988], p. 67.

2. The National Government had 556 supporters, including 472 Conservatives, as opposed to 46 members of the Labour Party and I.L.P. Mowat, pp. 411-412.

3. The Liberals supporting the National Government [four "Lloyd George Liberals" were in opposition from the election on] split over the policy of tariffs in September 1932. Samuel led half into opposition, Simon led the half [National Liberals] which remained.

4. Taylor, 1914-1945, p. 351.

5. Canada, Australia, New Zealand, the white-controlled colonies of Rhodesia and South Africa, and, to a lesser extent, Ireland.

6. Taylor, 1914-1945, pp. 357-358.

7. The Indian debate alone took over four years, and took up more time in that period than any other issue.

8. Mostly because the General Election put the focus on the Abyssinian Crisis.

9. Basically, the 10 year rule was a Cabinet decision that there was no reason to suppose that there was any chance of Britain becoming involved in a large scale war during the following ten years. The rule was reviewed every year by the Cabinet.

10. Robert Paul Shay, Jr., British Rearmament in the Thirties [Princeton, 1977], pp. 22-23.

11. Ibid., pp. 25-26.

2. Raymond J. Sontag, A Broken World [New York, 1971], p. 245. Even the workers building the League offices in Geneva could not bring themselves to believe in the League, Gibbs, pp. 106-107. For a good summary of the disillusionment that the failure to disarm caused to its supporters, see Berkman, pp. 147-156.

3. Hugh R. Wilson, Diplomat Between the Wars [New York, 1941], p. 268.

4. Germany and Italy were not interested in putting any real power into League hands, as that could have discouraged any attempts to revise the Versailles Treaty. French politicians tended to regard the League mainly as a means to keep Germany in its place, and had no political interests [imperial or economic] in Northern China to override that position. For Britain, Japan had been a traditional ally for the previous quarter century, and a possible ally against any Soviet expansion in Asia. The Soviets had been clashing with the Chinese in Mongolia and also had claims in Manchuria. Of the two, Japan was viewed as preferable.

15. A.J.P. Taylor, The Origins of the Second World War [New York, 1966], p. 64.

16. Ibid., p. 63.

17. Shay, p. 32.

18. Ibid., pp. 33-37.

19. Attributed to Baldwin by Shay, p. 37, although his citation does not bear him out, and by Kenneth Rose in King George V [New York, 1984], p. 386, without citation. This view is echoed by Beverley Nichols in Cry Havoc! "There is hardly a single living authority who attempts to deny that the next war will be largely decided in the air, and that the first and main object of any air force will be to paralyze the enemy's nerve centers—i.e., to destroy the chief enemy towns." p. 24. See also Wagar, p. 124.

20. For the text of Churchill's speech, see Parliamentary Debates, volume 285, columns 1193-1200, Baldwin's reply, columns 1200-1208.

21. Quoted by Shay, p. 38.

22. See Manchester, pp. 208-210 for some interesting observations on Chamberlain's preference for a strong [i.e. balanced] budget over a strong defense.

23. The first four questions were:
    1) Should Great Britain remain a member of the League of Nations?
    2) Are you in favour of an all-round reduction of armaments by international agreement?
    3) Are you in favour of the all-round abolition of national military and naval aircraft by international agreement?
    4) Should the manufacture and sale of armament for private profit by prohibited by international agreement?

24. Berkman, pp. 224-225.

25. P. M. H. Bell, in his excellent little summery The Origins of the Second World War In Europe [London, 1986], dismisses the fact in a clause [p. 102], and yet the Peace Ballot is the main evidence given for his belief in British support for the League and disarmament [pp. 101-103].

26. Mowat, p. 544. These papers cover the political spectrum fairly well.

27. Some of the items listed for the boycott were camels, mules, and aluminum–the last named one of Italy's major exports at the time. Manchester, p. 162. For Manchester's account of Hoare-Laval, see pp. 160-166.

28. The new National Government had a majority of 247. Mowat, p. 554.

29. Chamberlain had a majority of 81. Parliamentary Debates, volume 360, columns, 1361-1366.

30. Origins, p. 101.

31. Ibid., pp. 99-100.

32. A.L. Rowse, <u>Appeasement: A Study in Political Decline, 1933-39</u> [New York, 1961], p. 39; see also p. 14.

33. <u>Origins</u>, p. 97-99.

34. <u>Ibid.</u>, pp. 100-101.

35. <u>Ibid.</u>, p. 101.

36. Manchester, p. 176.

37. John, Viscount Simon, <u>Retrospect</u> [London, 1952], p. 202.

38. Manchester called the Naval Treaty "an offer which any proud government would have rejected." p. 144. See pp. 144-148.

39. Samuel, Viscount Templewood [Hoare], <u>Nine Troubled Years</u> [London, 1954], pp. 135-148.

40. Hoare states [pp. 140-141] that the "French unofficially told us that we had better go ahead in the Naval Treaty without asking them for a formal answer." Needless to say, there is little, if any, evidence that the British consulted the French in any way. Hoare's contention that the Anglo-German Treaty was a part of the Naval Conferences of the 1920s [pp. 139-140] is also pure sophistry. His chapter, and to a lesser extent his book, is filled with such statements.

41. This seems to be Bell's point of view on British motives, pp. 103, 299.

42. Such an idea could be discussed, though. For example, take this conversation between Rowse and Geoffrey Dawson, the powerful editor of the "Times," who used the "Times" to support and, at times, push the policies of appeasement.

> [Rowse] "Look, can't you let up on your campaign against the Italians? It isn't <u>they</u> who are the danger. It is the German's who are so powerful...."

> Dawson replied "To take your argument on its own valuation–mind you, I'm not saying that I agree with it–but if the Germans are so power-ful as you say, oughtn't we go in with them?" [All italics Rowse's.]

43. John Ehrman, Cabinet Government and War 1890-1940 [Hamden, Connecticut, 1964], pp. 112-113.

44. The first quote is Mowat, pp. 573-574; the second, Origins, p. 122.

45. Ibid., pp. 121-122.

46. Ibid., p. 121.

47. An attack just on France was thought impossible in 1938 because of French alliances with the U.S.S.R., Czechoslovakia, and Britain. An attack on the Low Countries would result in the same alliance system as an attack on France. An attack on Poland was at first believed unlikely, because Polish power was overestimated in the West [and in Poland]. Czechoslovakia had alliances with France and the Soviets, strong forward bases near the German heartland, and the most modern mechanized army in the world. If Austria was taken over, however, Czechoslovak defenses would be outflanked.

48. For Eden's version of his resignation, see his Facing the Dictators [Boston, 1962], pp. 621-689. It is also one of the most detailed accounts.

49. For a brief outline of Anglo-Japanese relations between 1934-1941, see Malcolm D. Kennedy, The Estrangement of Great Britain and Japan [Berkeley, 1969], pp. 316-345.

50. Sir Horace Wilson to Leonard Moseley, in Moseley's On Borrowed Time [New York, 1969], pp. 22-23.

51. Ibid., p. 23.

52. Quoted by Mowat, p. 615; Manchester, p. 348. Chamberlain made

that statement on September 27, 1938, at the very height of the crisis, in response to one of Hitler's nastiest speeches condemning Czechoslovakia.

53. In the longer term, however, Czechoslovakia suffered less during the Second World War than Germany or Poland.

54. Origins, pp. 131-134.

55. Rowse, p. 19.

56. Hitler broke the Munich agreement when he took over the Czech state in the spring of 1939.

57. For fear of being defenseless, with no faith in the League or any international agreement.

58. Rowse, p. 20.

59. Ibid.

ACCEPTING APPEASEMENT

Why did the leaders of the National Government believe Hitler could be or should be appeased at Munich? Why did the British public cheer the results of the Munich Conference? How did the appeasers justify their policies? In many respects, these questions are unanswerable. Each is so complex that it would take many scholars many volumes to even try and answer them. Telford Taylor took 1004 pages just to write a general narrative outline of appeasement,[1] and A. J. P. Taylor used 278 pages in order to suggest some theories of the causes of the war which followed appeasement.[2] The literature of appeasement is vast; British appeasement alone has generated such a large body of secondary material that every plausible [and many an implausible] theory has been covered in some manner.[3] No one has answered any of the above questions with any degree of acceptance from the historical profession, and I cannot claim to answer them. Rather, the interface between the third and fourth questions will be looked at, in light of the material presented in the previous chapters.

The interface between those two questions lies in the area of popular opinion. The crowds of people who cheered Chamberlain's return from Munich's connection with public opinion should be obvious,[4] while the connection with the appeasers' justification of appeasement will be made clear from the appeasers' memoirs.

There are easy answers to the third question; why the crowds cheered Chamberlain after Munich. One would be that the crowds were not fully aware what they were cheering. That is, the majority of the public was unable to form a critical understanding of the policies of appeasement because most of their information about those policies came from the appeasers themselves, filtered through the very co-operative British press,[5] and there is more than a possibility that those policies were based more on hopes than facts.[6] In short, for the casual followers of British foreign policy, it would be very difficult to distinguish between the pronouncements of their Government leaders and the realities of the situation.

Had there been any sort of unified anti-appeasement front in Britain, the British public may have had a more realistic appraisal of the European [and world] political situation in 1938. The truth of the matter was, however, that there was nothing like unity in the anti-appeasing ranks. The Labour Party was split between total pacifists, supporters of an underarmed collective security system still based on the League of Nations, and a few [mostly in the Parliamentary Labour Party] who were willing to support a limited rearmament; opposition outside the Labour Party in Parliament was limited to a few well-known individuals; and the press and intellectuals were split on foreign policy issues. The people who came out to cheer Chamberlain may have done so because their leaders had misinformed them about the issues of appeasement in general and the results of the Munich Conference in particular. So, even if those crowds of well-wishers were representative of the British public, here is no reason to assume those opinions would hold up once the excitement was over.

The modern historian should not, however, make the error of believing that the crowds who cheered Chamberlain after the Munich agreement were representative of public opinion during the years 1935-1938. It is tantalizing to speculate on what material would exist had the modern opinion poll been employed in Britain during the years of appeasement. One group of people were interested in the opinions of the public, however, and the results of a March 1938 poll taken by Mass Observation shows that the British public was confused about foreign policy, rather than supportive of the Prime Minister,[7] which was at least an improvement over the previous month.[8] In such a situation, it is not unreasonable to state the Government of the day was in a good position to mold public opinion, and Government opinion, after the departure of Eden, meant the opinion of Chamberlain. Telford Taylor, for one, holds strong opinions on Chamberlain and his duty:

> It has often and forcefully been argued that the state of public opinion and sentiment in Britain was such that the country would not have marshaled its resources or fought with determination in 1938, and that this became possible only after Hitler's destruction of the Prague Government....
> Proponents of this view point to Britain's long years of disarmament and peace; to the...counsel against war given by the military leaders; to the overwhelming support given Chamberlain by his Cabinet and party colleagues....
> Nevertheless...[t]he pronounced shift in public opinion during and after the Godesberg meeting,

resulting from Hitler's rejection of Chamberlain's proposals and from publication of Hitler's terms, showed that the British could be aroused to a high pitch of indignation; the subsequent general approval [of] Munich was given under the misapprehension that the Prime Minister had secured good terms....

Let us suppose that, after Godesberg, Chamberlain had told Britain and the Empire that...Hitler had reneged on the Berchtesgaden understanding and rejected these terms; that his word was not to be trusted...that the loss of Czechoslovakia's military capacity...would gravely affect Britain's security; and that unless Germany were checked Britain would confront a new...Napoleon—would not the island and the Dominions have understood and acted upon his warning? If the Prime Minister in his radio address to the nation in late September had trumpeted a fanfare instead of intoning a dirge, could he not have awakened his country to its peril? No doubt it would have gone to war grimly rather than ardently, but that was also the case in 1939. [9]

Yet to have done as Taylor suggests would have meant that Chamberlain would have had to totally rethink his opinions on foreign policy, and to admit that his critics had been correct about Hitler and Germany while he and his political allies had been wrong. Perhaps a more Machiavellian politician could have convinced the British public that he had just been waiting for proof of Hitler's bad intentions, or even made an admission of error followed by promises to mend the situation. Telford Taylor, however, knew that such behavior would have been

npossible for Chamberlain.[10] A. L. Rowse is always a good source for
pt remarks about the leading figures of the National Government, and
nmediately some of these remarks come to mind when the subject is
ne intellectual flexibility of those leaders.

> Yet they all thought lightly of Churchill: Baldwin
> was hostile to him, Neville Chamberlain thought
> that among all his many gifts, 'wisdom and judge-
> ment' were wanting. It was 'wisdom' to play
> Hitler's game, it was 'judgement' to make the way
> easy for him. [11]

If it is true that the leaders of the National Government were "dedi-
ated, with vast electoral majorities, to not letting the real issues pene-
rate through to the electorate,"[12] as much, if not all, the evidence
oints, then the great amount of talk bandied about by the appeasers
and their apologists about the state of public opinion in Britain being one
f the fundamental reasons for appeasement may be dismissed as a red
erring.[13] Evidence produced by Telford Taylor suggests that such evi-
lence on public opinion about appeasement there was cut both ways,
and that the leaders ignored it in any case.[14] Richard Cockett, in his
monograph on Chamberlain's relationship with the press, Twilight of
Truth, shows how Chamberlain may have even come to believe that his
own press releases reflected public opinion.[15] Finally, as Rowse put
t:

> what are political leaders for? Do we employ them
> to fall for the enemies of their country, to put

across to us the lies they are such fools as to believe?...the proper function of political leaders is
...not to be taken in, but to warn us. [16]

Three of the leading appeasers, Halifax, Simon, and Hoare, wrote very sanitized memoirs during the 1950s. Taking these three works, a-long with Keith Feilings' biography of Chamberlain–still the best biography of Chamberlain dealing with the appeasement years[17]–it is possible to see the image of appeasement which the authors of ap-peasement wished to put across, and how they defended themselves against their critics.

Feiling states that four legends have grown up around Chamberlain and his policies:

that he was always hostile to collective security,
that he was biased by sympathy to Germany, that
he ignored Russia, and that he impeded
rearmament. [18]

The second charge will not be discussed, as there is no evidence to suggest that Chamberlain had any feeling but dislike about the Nazi regime,[19] but an additional charge that the appeasers did nothing to educate the British public about the dangers of Nazi Germany, or the need for rearmament, and in fact used public opinion as their main scapegoat in excusing their policies, must be added.

The use the appeasers made of their concept of public opinion has been discussed. It is important, however, to see how they went about abusing the term "public opinion." Hoare, for one, makes good use of the term and concept when he was discussing the reoccupation of the Rhineland.

> [I] remember the general attitude both of the Government and the British public at the time.... "What justification could there be for a European war to uphold an out-of-date clause of the Versailles Treaty, and why should not the Germany have full sovereign rights in some of the most German territories of the Reich?" These were the questions that three people out of four were asking themselves. In view of this almost universal feeling, the Government would have little or no support for pressing...the French into war. [20]

Hoare did not, of course, think it necessary to show how he arrived at "three out of four," his memory was, in his opinion, good enough evidence. Nor has any later defender of Chamberlain been able to do more than make general statements, such as

> ...it does seem fairly certain that...at the time of Munich, the vague and ill-defined force known as public opinion was squarely behind the prime minister.... It is therefore no great exaggeration to say that the country lay in the palm of [Chamberlain's] hand. [21]

Although Hoare writes a great deal about public opinion, it is clear from the context that there was really no reaction from the Government

210

to Hitler's move, just as it is clear that the "out-of-date" clause was only dated when the French and British Governments failed to enforce it.

The extension of German Lebensraum through the Anschluss brought about a similar defense from Hoare:

> It was...evident that, deeply as both countries resented Hitler's brutal action, neither the British nor the French people were prepared to go to war to prevent German Austria from becoming part of the German Reich. [22]

In short, Hoare was able to ease his conscience in part by believing, or at least saying, that he and the other appeasers "acted in accordance with the view of...a large body of public opinion in the country."[23]

Lord Halifax, Foreign Secretary from Eden's resignation until the fall of Chamberlain's Government in 1940, provides an echo to Hoare.

> I have little doubt that if we had then told Hitler bluntly to go back, his power for future and larger mischief would have been broken. But...there was no section of British public opinion that would not have been directly opposed to such action in 1936. To go to war with Germany for walking into their own backyard, which was how the British people saw it...was not the sort of thing people could understand.
>
> No one who had the misfortune to preside over the Foreign Office at that time could ever for one moment of the twenty-four hours of each day forget that he had little or nothing in his hands with which to support his diplomatic efforts. The

British people had, through the years of wishful thinking, come to believe that because they so clearly recognized war to be a bad plan, everybody else must recognize it for such too. [24]

These men were also happy to put the blame for Britain's military unpreparedness on others as well, forgetting who it was who controlled the Commons from 1931 on, as well as during most of the 1920s.[25]

[T]here were...considerations...critics ought to ...regard. One was that in criticizing the settlement of Munich, they were criticizing the wrong thing and the wrong date. They ought to have criticized the failure of successive Governments, and of all parties, to foresee the necessity of rearming in the light of what was going on in Germany.... [26]

It was, of course, Halifax's party, and Chamberlain's and Hoare's, which controlled Parliament throughout this time period. Even though some later historians have tried to defend Chamberlain's record on the grounds that he supported [and fought for] the limited rearmament of the 1930s against a fair amount of opposition,[27] the fact remains that the rearmament program Chamberlain supported was totally inadequate for British defense needs in Europe, let alone Britain's imperial needs. [A more accurate view of British rearmament can be found in the previously cited British Rearmament in the Thirties by Robert Paul Shay, Jr.]

The most commonly cited instance of both public opinion regis-
tering opposition to any type of aggressive acts [such as rearming] and
of Labour Party obstruction of British rearmament was the 1933 by-
election in East Fulham, where a large majority for the Conservative-
Unionist Party candidate in 1931 was turned into a narrow majority for
Labour.[28] As two of the better-known early secondary sources put it:

> The Unionists' party conference was anxious
> about defense, but its leader asked it to think
> again, the Labour Conference pledged itself to
> have no hand in war, and...at East Fulham...[won
> a] victory, expressly on the theme of a war-
> mongering government.

> The [Times] was firmly settled in its belief that
> Germany was as willing as other countries to
> "settle down as good neighbors." There was no
> indication in 1935 or later that the office wishes to
> abandon the elan given by "public opinion" as
> registered, for example, in East Fulham.... The
> paper followed by the people.... [The editors], like
> the country, were determined to "forget all about
> the war." [29]

Hoare adds his opinion of the East Fulham election by crediting the
"pacifist wave" to public response to some of the pacifist statements he
claimed were made by the Labourites:

> "I am asking for votes for peace and disarmament;
> my opponent demands armaments and prepara-
> tions for war." "I would close every recruiting
> station, disband the army and dismiss the air

force. I would abolish the whole dreadful equip-
ment of war and say to the world, 'Do your worst
...."[30]

Telford Taylor, on the other hand, states that John Wilmot, the Labour candidate, "was a Navy veteran of the First World War and no pacifist, but he campaigned on a platform of collective security," and that East Fulham was a natural backswing in reaction to the 1931 General Election.[31]

It is A. J. P. Taylor, however, who must be turned to in order to get the East Fulham election viewed from an entirely different angle.

Neville Chamberlain suspected that at East Fulham "the main attack was on the means test," and
later investigation had confirmed his judgement.
Electors, as distinct from politicians, were interested in housing and unemployment, not foreign
affairs.[32]

The truth of the East Fulham election is hard to determine now, as it was hard to determine then. In any event, no matter what the cause or combination of causes for the turn around, there is really little doubt that the by-election upset some of the leaders of the National Government. Hoare, for example, states that Baldwin was "greatly shaken by the East Fulham result,"[33] and even A. J. P. Taylor says that

East Fulham frightened the government out of
what senses they had, Baldwin most of all.... The

government would have given a resolute lead, if they had seen clearly what lead to give. They did not. [34]

These last two sentences of the Taylor quote point out one of the main problem areas to scholars studying appeasement: appeasement was not a set policy, unless the desire to avoid war at almost any price can be called a set policy. Rather, appeasement was a set of improvisations, some ill-timed and ill-conceived [such as the Hoare-Laval plan] and some which looked brilliant at the time [such as Chamberlain's first trip to Germany]. Try as they sometimes did, the leaders of the National Government could not control events, since the only way, it turned out, they could have had any control over them would have been to acknowledge that the actions of the British Government would, in the end, have to be backed up by superior military power, and that the power would be used. When the British and the French had the superior power [up until the Munich pact], they refused to make any effective threat. Once the taking of Prague forced them to take a stand, the French and British no longer had any obvious military superiority.

It cannot be argued that the leaders of the National Government did not know, in general, what Hitler wanted. As the British Ambassador during the last years of appeasement, Sir Nevile Henderson, noted in his memoirs:

In the years between 1933 and 1938 it was a common question to hear, "What does Hitler really

want?" It had always been answered...in the same
sense: first, Austria, then the Sudetan Lands; and
after that, the liquidation of Memel, the Corridor,
and Danzig; and finally the lost colonies. From
the beginning of my mission I have never found
any reason to disagree with the accuracy of [that]
judgement.... [35]

Perhaps the main problem which the National Government had is best put in a comment from The History of the Times, as the word "paper" could easily be replaced by "Government" without any loss of meaning.

"Europe in fact is placed in the dilemma of having
to refuse to force what reason suggests should at
least in part be conceded, or else of yielding to
extremism what earlier was refused to modera-
tion." [from the Times of June 28, 1933].... For
six years the paper saw no reason why an action
that was justified by ethics and politics before
January, 1933, should be held to be falsified by
the events of the 30th of that month. [36]

If the editors of the Times, the leading conservative newspaper, who had close ties to the leading Conservatives and an extensive correspondent system[37] could not see how the Nazi system of government was different from either the Weimar government or the system of their French allies, it would be difficult not to see why many others in Britain were confused as well.

In fact, some members of the National Government apparently never saw that they had, at best, been incorrect in their opinions on foreign policy during the 1930s, or cared to admit that they had been wrong. Two of the leading members of the appeasing group, Hoare and Halifax, at least mentioned doubts. Halifax stated that

> [t]he criticism exited by Munich never caused me the least surprise. I should very possibly indeed have been among the critics myself, if I had not happened to be in a position of responsibility. [38]

Hoare was not able to go as far as Halifax's very veiled criticism of Munich, let alone the entire policy of appeasement. He at least refused to celebrate the Munich accords as victory, and, unlike Chamberlain, who disliked the Czechs, Hoare knew their leaders and liked them.

> Unlike some of my friends, I was profoundly depressed. I felt great sympathy for the Czechs. Their leaders had been my personal friends, and their country I had admired for many years....
> I...insisted that we were not celebrating a triumph. We had made our choice, not because it was good, but because it was less bad than the alternative....
> Deeply as I deplored the crushing blow to a loyal ally, I was satisfied that the Munich terms were definitely better than the conditions of the Godesberg diktat.... The critics were...to say that cold-blooded murder by installment was no better and perhaps worse than a sudden act of homicidal violence.... The next six months were to prove the critics right. [39]

Considering the point of view Chamberlain expressed about the Czechs [as given in the previous chapter], Hoare's view was almost enlightened. It should be remembered, however, that Chamberlain's view was closer to the majority view of most Members of Parliament.[40] It was Chamberlain whose opinion really counted, not Hoare's, and it was Chamberlain who was said to have told told the Czech ambassador to Britain [Jan Masaryk, son of the founder of Czechoslovakia] after Godesberg, "My dear Jan...some people trust Dr. Benes, I prefer to trust Herr Hitler."[41]

The essence of the arguments put forth by Halifax and Hoare would be that "we didn't know" [that is, the appeasers could not have known that Hitler would not stop his expansion and would not keep his word], and that "we couldn't do any more with what we had" [that is, public opinion and the Labour Party were immovable objects, preventing the Government leaders to be any tougher with Hitler than what they were already].

There are, however, signs that these two men knew, or at least suspected, that they had been wrong, and were just trying to justify to themselves the policies which had proved to have been the incorrect policies to follow. John Simon's memoirs, however, do not even have that additional hint that the policies he had supported were wrong.

At first glance, his memoirs seem to fit in with Halifax's and Hoare's, as with his own mention of how British public opinion could be gauged.

218

> Stanley Baldwin was the typical Englishman, the embodiment of the English ways, devoted to the English tradition above everything else in the world...and his instinct...led him to the conclusion which the ordinary man approved. [42]

And, of course, the slow course of rearmament was approved of in the famous lawyer's least offensive manner.

> At the time, Baldwin's moderation reflected the opinion of the country.... He was well aware of the need to rearm in the face of the growing German menace and he did set on...[increases] in our defensive strength, picking his way between Churchill's robust demands and the obsession of opponents who resisted increased estimates as ...a positive provocation of war. [43]

From what Simon, Hoare, and Halifax said in their memoirs, one might think that the National Government was a split, near-minority Government under heavy press attack, rather than a loyal group with a vast majority and a largely sycophant press. There is no more than a hint in Simon's memoirs that "Churchill's robust strength" might have been a better policy in the mid and late 1930s than his own Government's policy of slow rearmament, nor any suggestion that perhaps the world's last chance of true disarmament was frittered away, in large part, by Great Britain, France, and the United States when Simon himself was foreign secretary. In fact, the National Government's policy on arms might be said to have been a few too many arms to have disarmament and not quite enough arms to achieve security, done in the belief that British bonds would be more powerful than British bombers or bullets.

Simon's defense of Munich is the strongest to be found amongst the memoirs of the men responsible, and in putting what case he had in the strongest terms possible,[44] he showed why he was regarded as one of the best barristers of his generation. The chapter starts off with an attack, and the tone is maintained throughout the chapter.

> The Munich crisis of September 1938 affords a classic instance of how a high-minded and courageous man (for such Neville Chamberlain undoubtedly was) may take a course which for the time being brought him overwhelming messages of congratulation, only to find that, after the sense of general relief had passed, his effort is denounced as unworthy and pusillanimous, until the name of Munich in many mouths has become a byword. I held at the time, and have always held, that the Prime Minister's action was justified by the circumstances then existing and that the effort he made then should always be remembered in his honour. The fact that his action did not ultimately preserve peace does not, in my judgement, affect the essential rightness of his policy at the time. Even if the effort were to fail, it was still right to attempt it....
>
> These views of mine may not commend themselves to those who find it enough at this distance of time [1952] to sneer at the "policy of appeasement," as if there were something discreditable in a statesman going to great lengths in the effort to find peaceful solutions before deciding that there was nothing for it but to let millions of people be plunged into the misery of years of war. At any

rate, it is a relief to me to have the opportunity of defending my Chief, and I propose to set out, briefly and objectively, the considerations by which history may decide whether Chamberlain's course in the year before the last war began was not justified. [45]

A great deal of historical ink has been spent on showing why Chamberlain, "high-minded and courageous" as he might have been, was wrong in his policies, and why the great lengths to which he was willing to go in order to keep Britain, as opposed to Europe, at peace, were, at best, "discreditable," and more ink will not be added at this time. It must again be pointed out that the memoirs of the appeasers were mainly written to justify their policies, naturally, and so must be read very carefully for both internal inconsistencies and inconsistencies with known facts.

There is one thing which the three memoirists agree upon which seems to be born out by later research—no matter how much Hoare, Halifax, Simon, Wilson, Henderson, or any other member of the British Government or Foreign Service may have approved of appeasement, the one person most responsible for its course in Britain was Neville Chamberlain, especially after he became Prime Minister in the spring of 1937. [46]

It was no secret to any of us that, long before he became Prime Minister, he [Chamberlain] had fretted under the easy-going methods of Baldwin. Baldwin was not really interested in foreign affairs

> .... Chamberlain...had the most definite views as to what was needed.... [e]ven before he succeeded Baldwin, and when he was still Chancellor of the Exchequer.... [47]

Chamberlain went to deal with Hitler filled with the belief that he alone could deal with the German leader, and that belief seems to have been based on the twin convictions that Hitler was a person who could be reasoned with, while he was also a fanatic who had to be approached with caution.

> [Chamberlain] knew that he was dealing with an abnormal fanatic. It may be that his self-confidence misled him into thinking that the Fuhrer could be moved by arguments and explanations that seemed to us unanswerable. British Ministers...have always been inclined to act and think as if foreigners thought and acted like themselves.
>
> [There are] a large number of passages in Chamberlain's diary and letters to his sisters which reveal...his emerging self-image as the indispensable man, superior to any of his fellow ministers....
>
> Shortly before he became Prime Minister, Chamberlain told Lady Nancy "that he meant to be his own Foreign Minister." It was a comment which would have amused and perhaps alarmed brother Austen...who...was the elder statesman of British foreign policy, and who once...responded to [Neville] "Neville, you must remember you don't know anything about foreign affairs."

> [Chamberlain] had no belief in sudden inspira-
> tions or sensational short cuts: everything must be
> [done] patiently though out. Steady persistence
> —some might say obstinacy—in the course he had
> adopted was a strong element in his character.
> He had so often found the right solution, in mu-
> nicipal affairs or at the Treasury, by the hard
> labour of his own brains, that he was inwardly
> confident that world problems would in the end
> yield to his treatment.

> [Chamberlain] was so sure his plan was right, and
> so deeply convinced that he must carry it through
> without a moment's delay, that his singleness of
> urgent purpose made him impatient of obstacles
> and indifferent to incidental risks. [48]

Behind him, Chamberlain had a vast majority in the House of
Commons, which for the previous three hundred years had acted as the
main forum where opinion could be voiced on behalf of any political
opposition and the British people, and the majority of his colleagues in
the Cabinet. In the classic sense, Chamberlain had all the mandate he
needed for his policies, and under the British constitution, there was
nothing incorrect about Chamberlain's actions at any time unless he was
openly challenged by members of his cabinet.

As stated above, it is unfortunate from the modern historian's perspective that current practices of opinion surveys were just starting to be
employed in prewar Britain. It is also unfortunate that public opinion
could not be measured by the classic poll, the general election, which,
if war had not intervened, could only have centered on Chamberlain's

foreign policy. The next election did not have to occur until well into 1940, and for reasons only known to Chamberlain, he refused to call an election right after Munich itself.[49] It is possible that Chamberlain, who knew more about the Conservative Party organization than most, since he had created it,[50] believed that any election fought on the issue of Munich might have further split his Tory opponents from the main party, and, if they did better than some of Chamberlain's supporters, might have become a danger to Chamberlain's leadership.[51]

Chamberlain never abandoned his hopes for peace. Although the occupation of Prague in March, 1939, is often regarded as the end of appeasement, it did not end Chamberlain's quest for peace, as Hoare admitted in suggestive terms.

> As it was, Chamberlain's change of front in March, 1939, was accepted for what it really was, namely, a new move in his fight for peace, rather than a reversal of his peace policy. Hitler's entry into Prague was not, as many declared, the end of the peace policy. Chamberlain and his colleagues never abandoned the hope of preventing a world war until it actually broke out in September 1939. The lesson of Prague was not that further efforts for peace were futile.... [52]

Or, as Feiling said of Chamberlain:

> The difference between his critics and himself, though now much narrowed...was still there, turning on one plain fact; that, come what may, he would never accept war as inevitable. Neither at

home nor abroad would he do anything that might
bring it nearer, nor leave anything undone that
might stave it off.... If then his weapons had
changed, his purpose had not. [53]

For, as Chamberlain himself said: "I never accept the view that war is
inevitable."[54]

Chamberlain's main defense of Munich, and hence of his policies
of appeasement in general, were summed up in a speech he made after
the fall of Prague. The poor types of arguments which Chamberlain was
able to marshall in his defense show the low state which he had reached
by this time.

It has been suggested that this occupation of
Czechoslovakia was the direct consequence of the
visit which I paid to Germany last autumn, and
that, since the result of these events has been to
tear up the settlement...that proves that the whole
circumstances of those visits were wrong. It is
said that, as this was the personal policy of the
Prime Minister, the blame for the fate of Czechoslovakia must rest upon his shoulders. That is an
unwarrantable conclusion. The facts as they are
to-day cannot change the facts as they were last
September. If I was right then, I am still right
now. Then there are some people who say: 'We
considered you were wrong in September, and
now we have been proved right.'
Let me examine that. When I decided to go to
Germany I never expected that I was going to escape criticism. Indeed, I did not go there to get
popularity. I went there...because, in...an almost

desperate situation, that seemed to me to offer the only chance of averting a European war. And I might remind you that, when it was first announced that I was going, not a voice was raised in criticism. Everyone applauded that effort. [55] It was only later...that the attack began, and even then it was not the visit, it was the terms of settlement that were disapproved.

Well, I have never denied that the terms [of] Munich were not those that I...would have desired. But...I had to deal with no new problem. This was something that had existed since the Treaty of Versailles–a problem that ought to have been solved long ago if only the statesmen of the last twenty years had taken broader and more enlightened views of their duty. It had become like a disease which had been long neglected, and a surgical operation was necessary to save the life of the patient. [56]

After all, the first and the most immediate object of my visit was achieved. The peace of Europe was saved....

Really I have no need to defend my visits to Germany...for what was the alternative? Nothing ...could have saved Czechoslovakia from invasion and destruction. Even if we had gone to war to punish Germany for her actions, and if after the frightful looses which would have been inflicted upon all partakers in the war we had been victorious in the end, never could we have reconstructed Czechoslovakia as she was framed by the Treaty of Versailles.

But I had another purpose, too, in going to Munich. That was to further the policy...sometimes called European appeasement.... If that policy were to succeed, it was essential that no Power should seek to obtain a general domination

of Europe; but...should be contented to obtain
reasonable facilities for developing its own resources.... I felt that, although that might well
mean a clash of interests between different States
...by the exercise of mutual good will and understanding...it should be possible to resolve all differences by discussion and without armed conflict
.... I had some opportunities of talking with
[Hitler] and of hearing his views, and I thought
that results were not altogether unsatisfactory.

I do not believe there is anyone who will question
my sincerity when I say there is hardly anything I
would not sacrifice for peace...except...the liberty
that we have enjoyed for hundreds of years, and
which we will never surrender. [57]

Taking Chamberlain at his word, his justification for appeasement
is simple—anything which did not directly affect British liberty and
security could be sacrificed to preserve peace, since war would en-
danger that liberty and security. Abyssinia, Austria, Manchuria, and the
Sudetenland could be let go without any real struggle, and Prague taken
without any real protest, because Chamberlain did not believe them to
be necessary for British security, and there is no evidence to show that
Chamberlain ever regarded any of these areas vital, although arguments
over the importance of Austria and Czechoslovakia are argued still [the
many works cited in note 3 would be the best place to look for these
arguments].

Armaments and guarantees took the place of the openly appeasing
policies after the occupation of the rump Czech state, but, as stated

above, Chamberlain's policy was still peace, even if the weapons Chamberlain tried to use to maintain it were different. Hitler should be appeased, because he was correct in stating that all Germans [or at least most Germans] should be allowed, along with the territory they occupied, to be part of Greater Germany. This problem "ought to have been solved long ago," and there was "no reason why an action justified...before January 1933, should be held falsified by the events of the 30th of that month." Hitler could be reasoned with because "by the exercise of mutual good will and understanding...it should be possible to resolve all differences by discussion and without armed conflict," since "British Ministers...have always been inclined to think and act as if foreigners thought and acted like themselves," and Chamberlain "had formed decided judgments about all the political figures of the day...abroad, and felt himself capable of dealing with them."[58] Churchill finished an evaluation of Chamberlain in the following manner:

> His all-prevailing hope was to go down in history
> as the Great Peacemaker; and...he was prepared
> to strive continually in the teeth of facts, and face
> great risks for himself and his country. [59]

As Chamberlain went, so went the Cabinet, Parliament, and Britain's foreign policy.

But if the question of how the appeasers justified their policies can be considered answered [basically a combination of the pressure of "public opinion," Chamberlain's personal quest for peace, and the national Government leaders' version of the national interest], the

question of public opinion in relation to appeasement remains un-
answered. Unfortunately, there is very little concrete evidence about
British public opinion on foreign policy during the interwar period,
although the idea of public opinion was invoked throughout–especially
in relation to appeasement. This lack of concrete evidence has allowed
all those interested in the subject to project almost any set of opinions
onto the British public.

As far as public opinion and appeasement, the few famous instances of "British" opinion, such as the East Fulham election or the
Oxford Union debate,[60] which have been brought forward by the de-
fenders of appeasement to show that those policies were either supported by the public instances or forced the government to adopt those
policies because of them, are of dubious value not only because they did
not reflect any broad range of public opinion,[61] but, in this writer's
opinion, because they occurred before the 1935 general election, and
long before Germany's threat to peace was obvious. The closest thing
to a referendum on the policies of war and peace occurred in 1934-1935
[again before the main policies of appeasement were set] with the so-
called "Peace Ballot."[62] A great deal was made out of the fact that over
2,000,000 people had said that they were against the use of military force
[and about the same number had abstained],[63] but for some reason
the fact that over 6,000,000 [58.65%] of the respondents had said that
they would support military action was deemed irrelevant, both then and
later.

In short, there is really no evidence which shows that Telford
Taylor's conclusion about British determination–that Britain would have

gone to war in 1938 as they did in 1939, "grimly rather than ardently," should be disbelieved. Why then, were the appeasers able to invoke the specter of public sentiment at the time without being called on it?

One answer which has been suggested was the powerful pacifist movement of interwar Britain. Unfortunately, the formal pacifist movements are a nearly blind alley, as explained in Chapters V and VI. Many of the pacifists, such as Dick Sheppard and George Lansbury,[64] had powerful voices, but there is no evidence that any pacifist, group of pacifists, or pacifist group had any influence on British public policy. The pacifists' only real claim to influence came from the later apologists of appeasement, such as C. B. Pyper.[65] What has often been claimed as the pacifists' greatest victory–the Peace Ballot–in reality showed that well over half the people who responded [and most of the total number of respondents supported the League and were against large-scale armaments] were willing to have Britain fight any war "against aggression."[66] If there is any importance to be given to the pacifists, it is more because they existed than because of their activities.

The pacifists existed in the numbers they did because of the Great War. Very few of the "pacifists" actually were complete pacifists, but many more claimed to be "pacifists" in the sense of opposing war as an alternative policy because of the literature which came from the Great War, as well as contact with those who had similar experiences to the warriors/authors and shared their opinions. One such warrior/writer, Herbert Read, perhaps gave the strongest statement about the connection.

> War, thanks to the war books, was vivid enough
> .... But war acquires its reality from psychological
> and economic forces.... Our books may have
> created a few extra conscientious objectors, but in
> their main purpose, the prevention of another war,
> they had failed. [67]

Or, as an historian put it much later:

> Never again, many avowed upon concluding one
> of these books, would they participate in such a
> war. [68]

The role the pacifists played was similar to that of the warriors' literature: they made people aware of the possible problems and effects of war, and made sure that the possibility of war was always remembered. Had the political and diplomatic events which preceded the Second World War been more similar to those of the First, perhaps the pacifists would have had more influence. Despite the historians who have put World War II as the last act of a new Thirty Years War [or even a Hundred Years War between Germany and France], there were many differences between the events preceding the two world wars [the main one being while there was distrust, dislike, and competition between the two opposing camps before the Great War which allowed some responsibility to be thrown on everybody, before the Second World War, the main danger was clearly seen as Hitler]. In other words, where the danger to international peace was seen as the problems of the diplomatic system, the pacifists and internationalists seem to have had some influence [although not a great deal]. After the spring of 1938, as Hitler's demands became more and more strident, the pacifist movement began losing steam.[69]

It is probable that the pacifist movement was merely the best documented of the many manifestations of the climate of disillusionment which has been documented throughout this work, rather than an independent cultural movement. Outside of the realm of intellectual circles and some religious groups, there is little, if any, evidence of true pacifism. It was more of a feeling up and down the political spectrum that there was no reason good enough to repeat the horrors of the Great War. The British people were brought into the Great War on a great wave of patriotic fervor, which was sustained throughout the war [at least on the Home Front] by various types of propaganda. During the Second World War, the propaganda was much subdued, not as much made of atrocities [even though there were many more atrocities during World War II than World War I[70]] and the internationalist propaganda of the United Nations did not promise nearly as much as the League.

Despite all this, the British leaders still claimed public support for their policies, and used the crowds which flocked to cheer Chamberlain when he returned from Munich as proof–and that is all the proof that exists. Although there is no reason to suppose these crowds were representative of the whole of the British population, it must be admitted that they were spectacular. The appeasers believed these crowed were cheering the Munich accord, and Chamberlain built on this feeling when he made his "peace in our time" speech.

232

> My good friends, this is the second time in our
> history that there has come back from Germany to
> Downing Street peace with honour. I believe it is
> peace in our time. We thank you from the bottom
> of our hearts. [71]

If these crowds were cheering what Chamberlain believed they were, the historian may wonder at those who cheered for the destruction of another country and the increasing power of Hitler. The truth, of course, is that the British people had believed that they were going to be, within days, involved in another Great War, and those who cheered were rejoicing at the news that <u>they</u> were not going to be involved in a war so soon. How many believed that it was also "peace in our time" as opposed at those who were happy for a stay of execution is unfortunately impossible to even guess.

There can be little doubt that as the 1920s turned into the 1930s, the idea that there was a possibility of another great war turned into the probability that there would be one in the near future. Although many—perhaps even most—past generations have had some experience of war, very few have had the experience of total war. All Europeans over the age of thirty had this experience in some respect in 1938.

Again, all the European nations were affected, to a certain extent, by the warriors' literature, but it was the British who produced most of this literature during the interwar period [the most famous exceptions being Remarque and Hemingway]. As the chapter on Sayers pointed out, the type of experiences which the warriors had was seeping into the mainstream of British culture even before the deluge of warriors' work after 1928. These works, along with the diffusion of these works in the popular mediums of stage and film,[72] and those other works [such as those by Sayers] insured that the price paid in the field by those who fought in the last war could not be wholly forgotten as the next war approached. Other works, which have been briefly mentioned, fit in with the predictions of the politicians about the destruction of the next war. As was seen in Chapter IV, these memories and fears could not be counteracted by optimism in the general British society, because there was fairly little optimism to be had in interwar British society, especially in the 1930s. Although it cannot be shown to what extent the appeasers were affected by this general climate of disillusionment [at least until such time as the remaining papers and diaries of the appeasers are made available to the general historical community, if it is ever possible], it is certain that the appeasers were able to use the British fear of war–a fear caused, to a great extent, by the memories of the Great War–to insure acquiescence on the part of much of the British public to the policies of appeasement.

These policies were mainly the responsibility of one man, Neville Chamberlain, who was dedicated to his self-imposed mission, ignored the warnings of the Foreign Office, dominated his colleagues, and, to the last moment, refused to acknowledge he was wrong.[73]

The political destiny of Britain was controlled throughout the inter-war period by men like Chamberlain, who had some power during the Great War, but mainly made their careers during the 1920s. It may be possible that there was no connection between the political success of the appeasers, their foreign policies, and the climate of disillusionment which existed throughout the main portion of their political careers, but it is unlikely.

At this point, however, the most which can be said is that there existed in interwar Britain a climate of disillusionment and anti-militarism. The latter was caused by the experiences of the Great War, and the former was blamed on the Great War even though partially caused by other factors. This climate of opinion is intertwined with appeasement, and this was noted both by contemporary social and political historians writing before and after World War II as well as by the appeasers themselves. Until this time, although often remarked upon, this climate, its causes and possible effects, had not been explored in any detail. This does not pretend to be the definitive study of this climate of disillusionment, but one of the first studies.

NOTES

1. Telford Taylor, <u>Munich The Price of Peace</u> [Garden City, New York, 1979].

2. <u>Origins</u>.

3. Besides the works cited in the first two notes, some of the works used as background [which do not represent the whole of the field] include Keith Middlemass' <u>Diplomacy of Illusion</u> [London, 1972] [American title, <u>The Strategy of Appeasement</u>]; Martin Gilbert's <u>The Roots of Appeasement in the 1930's</u> [London, 1977]; William R. Rock's <u>Appeasement on Trial</u> [N. P.: Archon Books, 1966]; Martin Gilbert and Richard Gott's <u>The Appeasers</u> [Boston, 1963]; Thomas Jones' <u>A Diary with Letters</u> [London, 1954]; and Keith Middlemass and John Barnes' biography of <u>Baldwin</u> [London, 1969].

A number of other works helped establish the background of appeasement which, although not as important perhaps as the ones cited above, like them will not be cited elsewhere in this monograph. General works on foreign policy and appeasement include P.A. Reynolds' <u>British Foreign Policy in the Inter-war Years</u> [London, 1954]; Ritchie Ovendale's <u>'Appeasement' and the English Speaking World</u> [Cardiff, 1975]; Simon Newman's <u>March 1939</u> [Oxford, 1976]; W.N. Medlicott's <u>British Foreign Policy Since Versailles</u> [London, 1940]; Helen P. Kirkpatrick's <u>Under the British Umbrella</u> [New York, 1939]; David Dilks' [ed.] <u>Retreat From Power</u> [London, 1981]; Roy Douglas' <u>In the Year of Munich</u> [London, 1977]; Neville Waites' [ed.] <u>Troubled Neighbors</u> [London, 1971]; William J. Newman's <u>The Balance of Power in the Interwar Years</u> [New York, 1968]; John Connell's <u>The Office</u> [New York, 1958]; and Ian Colvin's <u>The Chamberlain Cabinet</u> [London, 1971]. Two flawed works on appeasement which are interesting because of their defence of Chamberlain are the decent <u>The Greatest Treason</u> [New York, 1968] by Laurence Thompson and the very flawed <u>Chamberlain and His Critics</u> [London, 1962] by C.B. Pyper.

Besides the small number cited, there are many works by and about those who were prominent in supporting or opposing appeasement. Some works about those who worked for appeasement in some way include Ramsay MacDonald by David Marquant [London, 1977]; Lord Lothian by J. R. M. Butler [London, 1960]; Lord Swinton by J. A. Cross [Oxford, 1982]; John Anderson by John W. Wheeler-Bennett [New York, 1962]; and The Diaries of Sir Alexander Cadogan O.M. 1938-45 [London, 1971], David Dilks ed. Some works by or about those who opposed appeasement include Leo S. Amery's My Political Life [London, 1953; Harold Macmillan's Winds of Change [New York, 1966]; Arthur, Lord Salter's Memoirs of a Public Servant [London, 1961]; Herbert, Viscount Samuel's Memoirs [London, 1945]; Alfred Duff Cooper's Old Men Forget [London, 1953]; Anthony, Earl of Avon's Facing the Dictators [Boston, 1962]; Anthony Eden [London, 1981] by David Carlton; Robert, Lord Vansittart's The Mist Procession [London, 1958]; Eugene Spier's Focus [London, 1963]; and Neville Thompson's The Anti-Appeasers [Oxford, 1971]. Although the above may seem a long list, it is only a small percentage of the total number of works in the subject.

4. At least the reception given to Chamberlain would indicate that the British public, at first glance, approved the idea of Munich. T. Taylor, pp. 63-65.

5. Exactly how cooperative the British press was in helping Chamberlain get his, and only his, point of view across to the general reading public [and the press was very cooperative] can be seen in Richard Cockett's monograph Twilight of Truth [New York, 1989].

6. "But [the appeasers] would not believe the facts themselves when they were given them—they preferred to lead the country, with continuous electoral success, in their illusions." Rowse, p. 12.

7. T. Taylor, pp. 830-831.

8. In February, the results to the question "Do you favour MR. Chamberlain's foreign policy" were: yes—26%; no—58%; No opinion—26%. Cockett, p. 190.

9. _Ibid._, pp. 992-993.

10. _Ibid._, p. 831.

11. Rowse, p. 56. See also p. 74.

12. _Ibid._, p. 831.

13. What often passed for "public opinion" was feedback, real or imagined, from the constituencies. See, for example, The History of the Times, Vol. IV, pt. ii [London, 1952], pp. 888-890. Again, it must be pointed out that the "free" British press was heavily influenced by the press office operated by Downing Street and other Government contacts with the press. See Cockett, especially p. 83.

14. T. Taylor, pp. 830-831.

15. Cockett, pp. 78-79, 87, 89, 90, 122-123.

16. Rowse, p. 58.

17. It is hoped that the second volume of David Dilks' biography of Chamberlain will soon appear. As this author said, in response to a survey taken by the journal Biography, Dilks' work "[w]ill become the standard biography for a long time to come, if finished." Biography, [Fall, 1985], p. 291.

18. Keith Feiling, Life of Neville Chamberlain [London, 1947], p. 250.

19. _Ibid._, p. 253. This charge may have been included by Feiling as a "strawman" argument.

20. Hoare, p. 201. See also Henderson, p. 124.

21. Larry William Fuchser, Neville Chamberlain and Appeasement [New York, 1982], p. 119.

22. Hoare, p. 283.

23. _Ibid._, p. 375. It must be remembered that Hoare was the main contact between Chamberlain and many of the newspaper editors

and owners, especially Lord Beaverbrook, and therefore he was well aware of the manipulation of the British press which gave a false impression of support for the policies of appeasement.

24. Edward, Lord Halifax, Fullness of Days [New York, 1957], The first quotation is from p. 200; the second, p. 198.

25. For example, see Hoare, pp. 12-21 and Feiling, pp. 312-318.

26. Halifax, pp. 199-200; but see Hoare, p. 381.

27. That is the main thesis of Fuchser's book, Neville Chamberlain and Appeasement.

28. The 1931 general election majority for the Conservative was 14,521, the 1933 by-election majority of the Labour candidate was 4,840. Mowat, p. 422. The Tory party is officially named the Conservative-Union Party. Unionists were not Labour people, but a group of Liberals, led by Neville Chamberlain's father Joseph, who favored continued union with Ireland. This split occurred 1886, and Chamberlain's father was a member of the Conservative Government of 1895.

29. The first quote is Feiling, p. 226; the second is from the History/Times, p. 895.

30. Hoare, pp. 126-127. There are, of course, no citations. The second quote is probably by the pacifist Labour leader George Lansbury, and as such is cited by T. Taylor, p. 204.

31. T. Taylor, p. 204.

32. Taylor, 1914-45, p. 367

33. Hoare, p. 127.

34. Taylor, 1914-45, p. 367.

35. Henderson, p. 130.

36. History/Times, p. 882. Other very powerful groups in Britain also had the same opinion. See Catherine Ann Cline, "Ecumenism and

Appeasement: The Bishops of the Church of England and the Treaty of Versailles" in The Journal of Modern History, volume 61 number 4, December 1989, pp. 683-684.

37. History/Times, pp. 882, 908-909.

38. Halifax, p. 199.

39. Hoare, p. 322.

40. The Czech ambassador to Britain in 1938 complained to a British friend that his country often called 'Czechslavia' or 'Czechoslovenia' in Parliamentary debates. Sir John Wheeler-Bennett, Knaves, Fools and Heroes [New York, 1974], p. 136. For the ambassador's reaction to Chamberlain's announcement he would go to Munich, see p. 140.

41. Ibid., p. 139.

42. Simon, p. 274.

43. Ibid., p. 275.

44. Simon, pp. 238-254.

45. Ibid., pp. 238-240.

46. Before becoming Prime Minister, Chamberlain's main responsibility would have been in supporting Baldwin and the National Government Foreign Secretaries [Simon, Hoare, and Eden] in their policies and in making certain that the price of rearmament did not go over the limits set by the Treasury.

47. Hoare, p. 291.

48. The first quote is ibid., p. 381. For an echo of the last sentiment in Chamberlain's own words, see the collection of his speeches In Search of Peace. The second quote is T. Taylor, pp. 552-53. Sir Austen died in 1937. The third quote is Simon, p. 278. The final quote is Hoare, p. 259. See also Winston S. Churchill, The Gathering Storm [New York, 1948], p. 199.

49. Feiling, pp. 384-385.

50. Hoare, pp. 376-377; Feiling, p. 177-179. See also Cockett, p. 8.

51. As Feiling, p. 384, noted, although small in number, the Tory dissidents were "highly officered."

52. Hoare, p. 377. Hoare, along with Halifax and Simon, were the colleagues.

53. Feiling, p. 402

54. Quoted by Feiling, p. 401.

55. Perhaps no voice was raised against the first and second trips [Berchtesgaden and Godesberg] because Parliament was not in session at the time. Nor did everyone applaud the announcement of the trip to Munich. Harold Nicolson, Diaries and Letters 1930-1939 [New York, 1966], p. 371.

56. Meaning Europe, it is hoped, not Czechoslovakia.

57. Chamberlain, pp. 270-272, 274-275.

58. Gathering Storm, p. 199.

59. Ibid.

60. The Oxford debate was on whether "this House will, in no circumstance, fight for King and Country," and which passed by a vote of 275-153 in the Oxford Union February 9, 1933.

61. That is, the by-election in East Fulham was not as important as a general election, and the Oxford debate was, in theory, decided on the merits of the debate, not the question itself.

62. For a good general account, see Berkman, pp. 214-237.

63. Ibid., p. 225; Hoare, pp. 127-129; Feiling, pp. 262, 266; Mowat, p. 542.

64. See George Lansbury's _My Quest For Peace_ [London, 1938] for the best account.

65. See above, n. 3.

66. The definition of "against aggression" was up to the individual respondent.

67. Herbert Read, "The Failure of the War Books" in _A Coat of Many Colours_ [London, 1945], pp. 74-75.

68. Berkman, p. 104.

69. Berkman documents this decline [pp. 309-337], although she gives slightly different reasons for it.

70. On the bearing this will have on the Holocaust, see Walter Laqueur's _The Terrible Secret_ [Harmondsworth, England, 1980].

71. Chamberlain, p. 200.

72. Noel Coward, for example, was pressed into a performance of _Journey's End_ in Singapore while travelling through Asia in 1929, a rather quick diffusion. _Present Indicative_, p. 330.

73. Chamberlain, it must be remembered, continued trying to work for peace even after the invasion of Poland. For one account, see Manchester, pp. 525-540 and 582-586, for Chamberlain's actions during the outbreak of World War II. See also Cockett, pp. 165-183.

BIBLIOGRAPHY

Primary Sources: British Home Front and Propaganda

Bedier, Joseph, German Atrocities from German Evidence [Paris, 1917].

_____, How Germany Seeks to Justify her Atrocities [Paris, 1917].

Belloc, Hilaire, The Elements of the Great War [New York, vol. I, 1915; vol. II, 1916].

Bryce, Viscount James, Essays and Addresses in War Time [Freeport, New York, 1968].

Churchill, Winston S., The World Crisis [New York, 1924].

Clarke, George H., A Treasury of War Poetry [Boston, 1916].

Cunliffe, J.W., The Poems of the Great War [New York, 1916].

Dawson, Coningsby, Carry On [New York, 1917].

Hamilton, Lord Ernest, The First Seven Divisions [London, 1916].

Lauder, Harry, A Minstrel in France [New York, 1918].

Masefield, John, The Old Front Line [London, 1917].

Northcliffe, Lord, At the War [London, 1916].

Nothomb, Pierre, The Barbarians in Belgium [London, 1915].

Pollard, A.F., The War: its history and its morals [London, 1915].

Raemaeker, Louis, Raemaeker's Cartoons [Garden City, 1916].

Reports on the Violation of the Rights of Nations and of the Customs of War in Belgium [London, 1915].

Robertson, J.M., War & Civilization [London, 1917].

Russell, W.E., The Spirit of England [London, 1915].

Toynbee, Arnold, The German Terror in Belgium [London, 1917].

_____, The German Terror in France [London, 1917].

"X," War Poems of "X" [London, 1916].

Secondary Sources: British Home Front and Propaganda

Brown, Malcolm, Tommy Goes to War [London, 1978].

Lasswell, Harold, Propaganda Technique in the World War [New York, 1927].

Marrin, Albert, The Last Crusade [Durham, North Carolina, 1974].

Marwick, Arthur, The Deluge [Boston, 1955].

Read, James M., Atrocity Propaganda 1914-1919 [New Haven, 1941].

Roetter, Charles, The Art of Psychological Warfare 1914-45 [New York, 1974].

Rothwell, V.H., British War Aims and Peace Diplomacy [Oxford, 1971].

Sanders, Michael and Taylor, Phillip, British Propaganda at Home and Abroad 1914-18 [London, 1982].

Stromberg, Roland N., Redemption by War [Lawrence, 1982].

Turner, E.S., Dear Old Blighty [London, 1980].

William, John, The Other Battleground [Chicago, 1972].

What Did You Do In The War Daddy [Melbourne, 1983].

Contemporary Social Histories

Collier, John, and Lang, Ian, Just the Other Day [New York, 1932].

A Gentleman with a Duster [Harold Begbie], The Glass of Fashion [New York, 1921].

_____, The Mirrors of Westminster [New York, 1921].

_____, The Windows of Westminster [New York, 1924].

Graves, Robert, and Hodges, Alan, The Long Week-End [New York, 1963].

Muggeridge, Malcolm, The Thirties [London, 1940].

Orwell, George, The Road to Wigan Pier [New York, 1958].

Secondary Social and Interwar Histories

Berkman, Joyce, "Pacifism in England 1914-39" [Yale, 1967].

Branson, Noreen, Britain in the Nineteen Twenties [Minneapolis, 1976].

Cockburn, Claud, The Devil's Decade [New York, 1973].

Cox, C.B., and Dyson, A.E., The Twentieth Century Mind [London, 1972].

Cutford, Rene, Later than We Thought [Newton Abbot, Devon, 1976].

Fussell, Paul, Abroad [Oxford, 1980].

Margetson, Stella, The Long Party [Farnborough, 1974].

Marwick, Arthur, Britain in the Century of Total War [Boson, 1968].

Mowat, Charles Loch, Britain Between the Wars [Chicago, 1955].

Rowbotham, Sheila, Hidden From History [London, 1973].

Seaman, L.C.B., Life in Britain Between the Wars [London, 1970].

Sontag, Raymond J., A Broken World [New York, 1971].

Stevenson, John, British Society 1914-1945 [London, 1984].

Taylor, A.J.P., English History 1914-45 [Oxford, 1965].

The Warriors' Literature: Primary Sources

Aldington, Richard, At All Costs [London, 1930].

_____, The Complete Poems of Richard Aldington [London, 1948].

_____, Death of a Hero [Garden City, 1929].

_____, Road to Glory [London, 1930].

Blunden, Edmund, Poems 1914-30 [London, 1930].

_____, Undertones of War [London, 1928].

Brittain, Vera, Chronicle of Youth [London, 1981].

_____ , Testament of Youth [New York, 1970].

Carrington, Charles Edmund, A Subaltern's War [New York, 1972].

_____ , "Letter to Author' [May 29, 1985].

Chapman, Guy, A Passionate Prodigality [New York, 1965].

Congreve, Billy, Armageddon Road [London, 1982].

Dolden, A. Stuart, Cannon Fodder [Poole, Dorset, 1980].

Gibbs, Philip, Now it can be Told [New York, 1920].

_____ , The War Dispatches [Isle of Man, 1964].

Graves, Robert, Fairies and Fusiliers [New York, 1919].

_____ , Good-bye to All That [Garden City, 1957].

_____ , Over the Brazier [London, 1916].

Gurney, Ivor, Collected Poems [Oxford, 1982].

MacGill, Patrick, The Great Push [Dover, NH, 1984].

Macmillan, Harold, Winds of Change [New York, 1966].

Montague, C.E., Disenchantment [London, 1968].

Owen, Wilfred, The Collected Poems of Wilfred Owen (preface by
    C. Day Lewis) [London, 1964].

Read, Herbert, A Coat of Many Colours [London, 1945].

_____ , The Collected Poems of Herbert Read [London, 1966].

248

_____, In Retreat [London, 1925].

Rosenberg, Issac, The Collected Works of Isaac Rosenberg [London, 1979].

Sassoon, Siegfried, Collected Poems 1908-1956 [London, 1956].

_____, The Complete Memoirs of George Sherston [London, 1937].

Silkin, Jon (ed.), The Penguin Book of First World War Poetry [New York, 1981].

Thomas, Edward, The Collected Poems of Edward Thomas [Oxford, 1978].

Vaughn, Edwin Campion, Some Desperate Glory [New York, 1988].

The Warriors' Literature: Secondary Sources

Ashworth, Tony, Trench Warfare [London, 1980].

Bergonzi, Bernard, Heroes' Twilight [London, 1965].

Bonadeo, Alfredo, Mark of the Beast: Death and Degradation in the Literature of the Great War [Lexington, Kentucky, 1989].

Brown, Malcome, Tommy Goes to War [London, 1979].

Ellis, John, Eye-deep in Hell [New York, 1976].

Fussell, Paul, The Great War and Modern Memory [London, 1975].

Hager, Phillip E., and Taylor, Desmond, The Novels of World War I [New York, 1981].

Leed, Eric J., <u>No Man's Land</u> [Chambridge, MA, 1979].

Lloyd, Alan, <u>The War in the Trenches</u> [New York, 1976].

Macdonald, Lyn, <u>1914</u> [New York, 1988].

_____, <u>The Roses of No Man's Land</u> [New York, 1984].

_____, <u>They Called It Passchendaele</u> [New York, 1984].

_____, <u>Somme</u> [London, 1983].

Middlebrooke, Martin, <u>The First Day on the Somme</u> [New York, 1972].

Norman, Terry, <u>The Hell They Call High Wood</u> [London, 1984].

Press, John, <u>Poets of World War I</u> [Windsor, 1983].

Taylor, A.J.P., <u>A History of the First World War</u> [New York, 1963].

van Creveld, Martin, <u>Command in War</u> [Cambridge, MA, 1985].

Ward, A.C., <u>The Nineteen-Twenties</u> [London, 1930].

Wohl, Robert, <u>The Generation of 1914</u> [Cambridge, MA, 1979].

The Works of Dorothy L. Sayers

Sayers, Dorothy L., "Biographical Note," found in various editions of Sayers' detective fiction after 1935, including the paperback Avon edition of <u>Unnatural Death</u>.

_____, <u>Busman's Honeymoon</u> [New York, 1965].

_____, <u>Clouds of Witness</u> [New York, 1966].

250

_____, <u>Five Red Herrings</u> [New York, 1968].

_____, <u>Gaudy Night</u> [New York, 1968].

_____, <u>Hangman's Holiday</u> [New York, 1969].

_____, <u>Have His Carcase</u> [New York, 1968].

_____, "How I cam to invent the Character of Lord Peter" ["Harcourt Brace News," July 15, 1936].

_____, <u>In the Teeth of the Evidence</u> [New York, 1967].

_____, <u>Lord Peter Views the Body</u> [New York, 1969].

_____, <u>Murder Must Advertise</u> [London, 1959].

_____, <u>The Nine Taylors</u> [London, 1962].

_____, <u>Striding Folly</u> [Sevenoaks, 1972].

_____, <u>Strong Poison</u> [New York, 1958].

_____, <u>Unnatural Death</u> [New York, 1955].

_____, <u>The Unpleasantness at the Bellona Club</u> [New York, 1963].

_____, Whose Body? [New York, 1961].

Secondary Works on Sayers

Brabazon, James, <u>Dorothy L. Sayers</u> [New York, 1982].

Charney, Hanna, <u>The Detective Novel of Manners</u> [London, 1981].

Durkin, Mary Brian, <u>Dorothy L. Sayers</u> [Boston, 1980].

Gaillard, Dawson, Dorothy L. Sayers [New York, 1981].

Haycroft, Howard, Murder for Pleasure [New York, 1943].

Hitchman, Janet, "Introduction" to Striding Folly [Sevenoaks, 1972].

_____, Such a Strange Lady [New York, 1973].

Hone, Ralph E., Dorothy L. Sayers [Kent, Ohio, 1979].

Wilson, Edmund, A Literary Chronicle: 1920-1950 [New York, 1956].

Interwar Fiction

Coward, Noel, Plays [volumes One through Three [London, 1979].

Doyle, Sir Arthur Conan, The Complete Sherlock Holmes [Garden City, 1930].

Snow, C.P., The Search [New York, 1934].

Waugh, Evelyn, Brideshead Revisited [Boston, 1945].

_____, Decline and Fall [Boston, 1928].

_____, A Handful of Dust [Boston, 1934].

_____, Tactical Exercise [Freeport, NY, 1936].

_____, Vile Bodies [Boston, 1930].

Wodehouse, P.G., The Code of the Woosters [New York, 1975].

Interwar Nonfiction

Bryon, Robert, The Road to Oxiana [New York, 1982].

Croft-Cooke, Rupert, The Man in Europe Street [New York, 1938].

Churchill, Winston S., Great Contemporaries [Chicago, 1937].

Engelbrecht, H.C., and Hanighen, F.C., Merchants of Death [New York, 1934].

Freud, Sigmund, Civilization and Its Discontents [New York, 1961].

Gibbs, Philip, European Journey [Garden City, 1934].

Low, David, The Best of Low [London, 1928].

_____, Low Again [London, 1938].

The National Peace Council, Peace Year Book 1938 [London, 1938].

_____, Peace Year Book 1939 [London, 1939].

Nicolson, Harold, Small Talk [New York, 1957].

Parliamentary Debates of the House of Commons ["Hansard"].

Reed, Douglas, Insanity Fair [London, 1938].

Waugh, Evelyn, A Bachelor Abroad [New York, 1930].

_____, A Little Order [London, 1977].

Beverley Nichols

Nichols, Beverley, <u>All I Could Never Be</u> [London, 1949].

_____, <u>Cry Havoc!</u> [London, 1933].

_____, <u>For Adults Only</u> [London, 1932].

_____, <u>News of England</u> [London, 1938].

_____, <u>No Place Like Home</u> [London, 1936].

_____, <u>The Sweet and Twenties</u> [London, 1958].

Autobiographies, Memoires, Speeches

Amery, Leo S., <u>My Political Life</u> [London, 1953].

Anthony, Lord Avon, <u>Facing the Dictators</u> [Boston, 1962].

Arthur, Lord Salter, <u>Memoirs of a Public Servant</u> [London, 1961].

Chamberlain, Neville, <u>In Search of Peace</u> [New York, 1939].

Churchill, Winston S., <u>The Gathering Storm</u> [New York, 1948].

_____, <u>Step by Step</u> [London, 1939].

Cooper, Alfred Duff, <u>Old Men Forget</u> [London, 1953].

Coward, Noel, <u>Present Indicative</u> [New York, 1937].

Dilks, David. (ed.), <u>The Diaries and Letters of Sir Alexander Cadogan O.M. 1938-45</u> [London, 1971].

Edward, Lord Halifax, Fullness of Days [New York, 1957].

Henderson, Sir Nevile, Failure of a Mission [New York, 1940].

Herbert, Viscount Samuel, Memoirs [London, 1945].

John, Viscount Simon, Retrospect [London, 1952].

Jones, Thomas, A Diary with Letters [London, 1954].

Lansbury, George, My Quest for Peace [London, 1938].

Nicolson, Harold, Diaries and Letters 1930-1939 [New York, 1966].

Robert, Lord Vansittart, Lessons of My Life [New York, 1943].

_____, The Mist Procession [London, 1958].

Rowse, A.L., Appeasement: A Study in Political Decline [New York, 1961].

Samuel, Viscount Templewood, Nine Troubled Years [London, 1954].

Shirer, William L., The Nightmare Years [London, 1954].

Wheeler-Bennett, Sir John, Knaves, Fools and Heroes [New York, 1974].

Wilson, Hugh R., Diplomat Between the Wars [New York, 1941].

Biographies

Butler, J.R.M., Lord Lothian [London, 1960].

Carlton, David, Anthony Eden [London, 1981].

Cross, J.A., Lord Swinton [Oxford, 1982].

_____, Sir Samuel Hoare [London, 1977].

Feiling, Keith, Life of Neville Chamberlain [London, 1947].

Manchester, William, The Last Lion Winston Spenser Churchill Alone 1932-1940, [Boston, 1988].

Marquand, David, Ramsey MacDonald [London, 1977].

Middlemass, Keith, and Barnes, John, Baldwin [London, 1969].

Rock, William R., Neville Chamberlain [New York, 1969].

Rose, Kenneth, King George V [New York, 1984].

Seymour-Ure, Colin, and Schoff, Jim, David Low [London, 1985].

Wheeler-Bennett, John W., John Anderson [New York, 1962].

Appeasement and Foreign Policy

Bell, P.M.H., The Origins of the Second World War in Europe [London, 1986].

Birn, Donald S., The League of Nations Union 1918-1945 [Oxford, 1981].

Cline, Catherine Ann, "Ecumenism and Appeasement: The Bishops of the Church of England and the Treaty of Versailles" in The Journal of Modern History, volume 61 number 4, December 1989, pp. 683-703.

Cockett, Richard, Twilight of Truth [New York, 1989].

Colvin, Ian, The Chamberlain Cabinet [London, 1971].

Connell, John, The Office [New York, 1958].

256

Dilks, David (ed.), <u>Retreat from Power</u> [London, 1981].

Douglas, Roy, <u>In the Year of Munich</u> [London, 1977].

Fuchser, Larry William, <u>Neville Chamberlain and Appeasement</u> [New York, 1982].

Gilbert, Martin, <u>The Roots of Appeasement</u> [New York, 1966].

_____, and Gott, Richard, <u>The Appeasers</u> [Boston, 1963].

<u>The History of the Times</u> [London, 1952].

Kennedy, Malcolm D., <u>The Estrangement of Great Britain and Japan</u> [Berkeley, 1961].

Kirkpatrick, Helen P., <u>Under the British Umbrella</u> [New York, 1939].

Large, David Clay, <u>Between Two Fires</u> [New York, 1990].

Medlicott, W.N., <u>British Foreign Policy Since Versailles</u> [London, 1940].

Middlemass, Keith, <u>Diplomacy of Illusion</u> [London, 1972].

Moseley, Leonard, <u>On Borrowed Time</u> [New York, 1969].

Newman, Simon, <u>March 1939</u> [Oxford, 1976].

Newman, William, <u>The Balance of Power in the Inter-war Years</u> [New York, 1968].

Ovendale, Ritchie, <u>'Appeasement' and the English Speaking World</u> [Cardiff, 1975].

Pyper, C.B., <u>Chamberlain and his Critics</u> [London, 1977].

Read, Anthony, and Fisher, David, <u>The Deadly Embrace</u> [New York, 1988].

Reynolds, P.A., British Foreign Policy in the Inter-war Years [London, 1954].

Rock, Edward, British Appeasement in the 1930s [London, 1977].

Rock, William R., Appeasement on Trial [N.P.: Archon Books, 1966].

Shay, Robert Paul, Jr., British Rearmament in the Thirties [Princeton, 1977].

Spier, Eugen, Focus [London, 1963].

Taylor, A.J.P., The Origins of the Second World War [Garden City, 1979].

Taylor, Telford, Munich the Price of Peace [Garden City, 1979].

Thompson, Laurence, The Greatest Treason [New York, 1968].

Thompson, Neville, The Anti-Appeasers [Oxford, 1971].

Waites, Neville, Troubled Neighbors [London, 1971].

Other Works Cited

Dangerfield, George, The Strange Death of Liberal England [New York, 1935].

Ehrman, John, Cabinet Government and War [Hamden, CN, 1964].

Fussell, Paul, "Writing in Wartime: the Uses of Innocence" lecture delivered October 26, 1983, SUNY at Binghamton.

Johnson, Paul, A History of the English People [New York, 1985].

_____, Modern Times [New York, 1983].

258

Lafore, Laurence, The Long Fuse [Philadelphia, 1971].

Laqueur, Walter, The Terrible Secret [Harmondsworth, England 1980].

Thompson, Richard S., The Atlantic Archipelago [Lewiston, NY, 1986]

Wagar, W. Warren, Terminal Visions [Bloomington, 1982].

INDEX